Tonya Raines

Copyright 2021 Tonya Raines
All rights reserved. No part of this book may be reproduced or used in any manner without the prior written consent of the copyright owner, except for brief quotations for book reviews.
To request permission, contact the publisher at tonya_raines@outlook.com.
ISBN: 978-0-578-86921-6
Printed by IngramSpark.com in the USA
Keystone Publishing
1950 S Scenic Ave
Springfield MO 65807
Tonyaraines.com

Milly-
    God wants you to know you are amazing to him. He is inviting you to go on a journey. You wont regret it!
Love
  Tonya

Table of Contents

Chapter 1	Broken Believers	1
Chapter 2	The Gift of Completeness	27
Chapter 3	Divine Love	48
Chapter 4	Your Journey is Real	65
Chapter 5	Grabbing Ahold of Your Future	93
Chapter 6	The Helper	114
Chapter 7	Weapons of a Warrior	130
Chapter 8	The Prayer of Permission	162

Introduction

This book is for you. I unknowingly began writing this book shortly after receiving salvation. You see, journaling has always been a practice of release, a place to store my thoughts, and a place to remember my thoughts. So, as a new Christian, it was very natural for me to write what I was reading in Scripture and learning from other believers. With hindsight, I understand what I did not then; God opened my heart and mind for believers stuck in a trial, temptation, or unbelief. Almost immediately, a message of hope began resonating within my spirit. I believe God positioned me to speak a message of hope to their confusion. In this book, you will find equal parts of truth-telling and hope.

The Lord prompted me to write this message because He earnestly wants you to know Him and become who you were always meant to be. Do not be surprised if you have to put this book down to allow your mind and heart to absorb what you are reading. You may feel provoked or even angry—that is completely acceptable. I promise one thing, if you hold on until the end, you will be different. In many ways, you will learn what I did.

I believe God brought you to this very moment because He wants to show you how much He loves you and has amazing plans for you. The purity of God's love exists perpetually, in a constant state. We, the body of Christ, spend our existence reconciling our inferior reality for the purity of God's love. Over the years, I have crossed paths with many broken believers who are drifting. They believe but are often suspended in their confusion without a clear understanding or pathway back into the arms of the Father.

As you find yourself in the pages of this book, you will be inspired, encouraged, and challenged to let go of the past and grab a new future. You will be equipped as the beautiful and empowered woman God designed you to be. The Drift is a message of grace and an invitation to reunite with the Father. Having prayed to have eyes to see people the way Jesus does, He gifted me with a depth of understanding about you. This book is for *you*. It is a divine message through my writing, straight from the Father's heart to you. He sent Jesus to us as an earthly king who leaves the ninety nine to find the one. He relentlessly pursues you even now, through your confusion and pain. I know because He pursued me for forty-four years. It does not matter what you have done or what you believe you have lost; He eagerly awaits your return.

My prayer for you is to have the courage to turn the pages and see yourself in it. There is healing here, with a message of love and unification. There is no greater love than that of our Heavenly Father. His desire is for you to be within the perfect environment of his love. May you begin this journey as a broken believer and finish as the warrior God created you to be.

Acknowledgements

It is quite humbling to pause momentarily and consider how you arrived at a particular moment and those around you who helped make it possible. I'm thankful for those who have gone before me as pioneers in ministry, self-publishing, and entrepreneurship. You have made my journey toward achievement much simpler. To those who invested time in discipling me as a new believer, thank you so very much. One sweet saint, in particular, Barbara Brown, was always so encouraging to me. She motivated my heart, and if she were here on earth right now, she would be beaming with excitement. I hope I can do for others what you have done for me, Barbara!

To all the friends who also have big ideas—not once did you discount mine. Thank you! To Skinner Virtual Services, the best developmental editing partner a first-time author can have. To AstroLogan Productions for always coming through, your work on the final cover was amazing! To the beta readers who prayed and gave me great encouragement and valuable feedback. In some ways, your fingerprint is on this book. Thank you!

Finally, I would like to dedicate this book to my family. Many have since left this earth, yet their impact and imprint shaped me into who I am and for each one of them I am grateful. To my children who have my heart, siblings, and mother, I bless you with the courage to discover what God has for you. I love you with all my heart.

Chapter One

Broken Believers

"Broken believers" have walked in salvation and faith, but at some point, you gave into temptation, trial, or unbelief. From this point, your story often becomes a domino effect of drifting away. You feel like you have to get yourself together and *then* come back to God. The reality is, as hard as you try, you cannot do it without Him. Broken believers often allow their own mistakes, or the mistakes of others, to get in the way of a relationship with Jesus. In fact, every follower of Christ can experience a broken believer phase. It can happen more easily than we think. Like you in this very moment, they reach a point of complete discontentment, not really knowing what to do.

You know there has to be a better way, a way that does not involve continually striving for salvation or frequently pushing the reset button on your faith journey.

This book was written to help you overcome everything that has or will set itself against your understanding of who you truly are. It will equip you with new insight and truth bombs that can improve your chances of a successful faith journey, a life full of peace, hope, and joy. You may be a broken believer now, but if you go on this journey and let this book be a guide, you will not be the same when you finish. You cannot walk with Jesus and remain the same. My prayer for you is to embrace your identity as a child of God and remain there into maturity.

Your salvation experience is not to be questioned from this point forward. The moment you asked Jesus into your heart was real. Side note: If you have not yet done this, please continue reading and open yourself up to the possibility of an amazing life as a child of God.

That initial connection with Jesus continues to carry meaning, even at this moment, as you read this. Despite what you believe or have been told, you received salvation. The resonance glory of Heaven touched your spirit. Now, you are eternally connected to God. He wants you to know he quickened you at that very moment. Since God's character is unfailing, He cannot lie, nor can he go against His word. Therefore, creating a foundation of trust, you begin to trust what He says and who He is. Trust is a Heavenly currency. Anyone who confesses with their mouth and believes in their heart that Jesus is Lord and Savior will no longer be bound to the grip of sin and have eternal life.

I know sin and eternal life are probably the last things on your mind; they were for me. I used to say, "that's nice, but what about my present? What about the genuine difficulties I am currently facing? In my beginning, I was going through a divorce; I was the primary caregiver and parent to three teenagers who were also struggling. I was a mess on the inside—a hot mess! There was no doubt I had experienced salvation, but I was in this place of being tapped out with conventional counseling and therapy. They helped, but it was not enough for me; I still needed healing. I went to church as a child and knew who God and Jesus were, but those memories were so far away and had been for years!

    I decided to give Jesus a try when it seemed I had exhausted all other options. Without writing another book, I can tell you I began to hear a message of hope for my broken family and me through the process of studying the Bible and learning who Jesus is. I learned about a love that transforms from the inside out; joy, not just happiness, was a real possibility. Most significantly, a life of hope and peace were gifts available to anyone who wanted to receive them. I felt like I had nothing to lose and, if it was true, a whole new life to gain. Over the years, the possibility became a reality. I moved from being a person of doubt, hopeless about my future, as I consistently let life happen to me, to carrying holy confidence in God.

My faith journey has not been a straight line marked by sterile benchmarks of growth, but I lack nothing. With each twist and turn, God has been faithful to meet me right where I was, in whatever emotional or mental state I was in, and guide me back to His truth. There is no perfection in the faith journey. As you progress in yours, please remember there is grace for your mess-ups. I messed up numerous times. In the moments of complete surrender, when I gave God my failures, I experienced mercy and grace followed by more understanding of His truth.

Over time, I noticed I was different, more patient, and focused on my new identity. You will transform as well. Do not forget to celebrate the small successes as you grow and learn. Each victory will build on the next. In the next section, you will read about the most common emotional-mental barriers that broken believers experience. As you read and begin to identify yourself with a particular barrier, ask yourself where you have been believing a lie and ask God to show you His truth. It may seem unnatural at first. The reality is, He deeply desires to develop a relationship with you, in truth and love.

Doubt is the first party crasher

What happens when your salvation moment fades, and you return to your real life, where everything is challenging? How do you react when you follow Jesus and mess up? What's next when you believe, but go back to the wilderness of a low paying job, complicated relationships, and dusty bank account? It seems as though doubt is the first on the scene with a straightforward question "Did that *really* happen, or was it something you made up in your head?"

In later chapters, you will learn about spiritual attack. For now, I need you to understand we have a defeated enemy I liken to a bully. Think back to your high school days and get a picture in your mind of who the bully was. Now recount how it appeared they had such authority. Everyone was afraid of this bully because they seemed to have all the control, fueled by an overinflated sense of insecurity. They made you doubt any success you had, and any achievement crumbled under their harsh words.

Satan is the spiritual bully. Throughout the rest of this book, I will refer to him as a bully. He really is a defeated bully; Jesus took care of that for us. The bully comes at us with lies about an inferior reality and deceit that keeps us from knowing the real truth because that is all he can do. He is powerless to take away what God has portioned for your life. As you return to the Lord, you are most susceptible to the bully's tactics—especially doubt. If he can cause you to doubt, his work is done. Meanwhile, you remain trapped. Maya Angelo was known to say, "when you know better, you do better." Now you know there is a bully in your life. As you gain a greater understanding of God's truth and about yourself, you will gain strength.

The truth you will gain will allow you to stand up against the bully. What if this truth lifts the veil from your face to let you see just how powerful you are in Jesus? Wouldn't you want to refuse doubt in favor of a life far greater? What if I told you that *you* are a threat to the bully? What if you hold power and authority he forfeited? The more you pursue Jesus, the more you will desire the greater reality of this faith journey. Every thought in your mind, give it to God in prayer and ask Him to give you His truth and peace.

Confusion & Distraction

If doubt is the first party crasher, confusion and distraction are the party guests who posse up with the bully and stay too long. **With his limited arsenal, the bully** loves to manipulate through confusion and distraction around the truth that God has declared. The veil of confusion and distraction comes in the form of temptation, trials, non-belief, and exertion of our will. Their assignment-keep you from realizing God's truth.

God's Voice	Satan's voice
Stills you	Rushes you
Leads you	Pushes you
Reassures you	Frightens you
Encourages you	Discourages you
Comforts you	Worries you
Calms you	Obsesses you
Convicts you	Condemns you

This illustration is simple yet profound. I want to encourage you to create your version and place it somewhere you will see it daily. You can begin to train your brain and your heart to listen correctly. I want to give you permission to disagree with any voice, not from God. As thoughts come into your mind, using this chart, you will begin to take every thought captive, and confusion will flee.

Imagine you and a friend are in a street side cafe having a conversation. As long as you are focused on what your friend is saying, there is complete clarity in the conversation. However, when you look away to notice a stranger walking by, you lose track of the conversation and become distracted. As long as you are fully engaged, you get it. When you take even a slight quarter-turn away from Him, you become distracted. A simple distraction can be all that is needed to keep you from knowing God's truth. It is naive to think it could be that straightforward, but his limited arsenal has a few perfected tools that the bully has used for centuries. Hopefully, this will enlighten you to see what is really happening.

You may have a promise from the Lord, and an opportunity presents itself that appears to be aligned. Confusion and distraction grow as you attempt to force a square peg into a round hole. If we are not careful, a tipping point occurs. The soul is a very powerful part of a human being. It wants what it wants. When we allow the soul to lead, it will try to fill our heart's desires IN OUR OWN STRENGTH, forsaking God's love and will. This tipping point can drag us back into negative behaviors of self-defeat.

To summarize here, the bully provokes our emotional weaknesses in an attempt to keep the soul veiled from the real truth. Are you ready to be free? Then let's keep building on the truth by learning the four ways broken believers can fall away.

Slow fade of temptation

Temptation is a deception that disguises itself as everything you think you want. It appears in the most appealing form. It can even be masked as something from God. The drift happens when someone falls into the trap of the deception that temptation offers. It does not just happen in one event. Although we can often look back to one event to understand what we could not see in hindsight at the moment. History always tells a different story than at any moment in time. Instead of a flashpoint event, a slow fade occurs. Broken believers try to hold on to the deception as if it were for them. Once the deception is exposed, shame comes to greet them. Shame clings to every thought, like a guest who will not leave at the end of an extended visit. Shame tag teams with doubt to leave the person weary. The world today is lit with constant temptation and pressure to conform to a highly self-centered existence.

The warning then and now is clear; be careful where you stand. Guard your heart and mind against the deceptive snare of temptation, especially since we are prone to it. What I mean by this is, as fallen humans, we are inclined to meet our own needs because, at some level, it works. The bully batters our soul, which seeks to meet its own needs. Opportunity can come dressed to the nines as everything you think you desire when its true purpose is to keep you separated from God. As new creations, we are given power and strength—from the Holy Spirit—to resist. Each time you resist and the temptation recedes, you weaken the enemy's ability to bully you.

Remember this as you continue reading. Your spirit was redeemed at salvation. Your soul is restored over time, and in relationship, with the Father. In other words, when we resist temptation, we align the soul with God's will for our lives, to understand that His ways are better than ours. The next time temptation subtly begins, you can learn to recognize it for all of its ugliness, and you can choose to send it packing!

Trials

Trials need to be thoroughly assessed through a spiritual lens and in fellowship with other believers. Some give credit to other people or the bully when it is God. Blaming your circumstances on others or suggesting the bully is "after you" when it is God can lead you down the wrong path. As believers, our faith will be tested. The faith journey you are on is not a single destination. It is a lifelong adventure of becoming. This means you have to train for your next destination continually. Do not confuse it with punishment. James 1 tells us to consider it joy when we encounter trials. Through the trials, we develop perseverance and maturity in Christ. Problems test who we are in Christ and what we believe about God. There will be times in your life when you will be tested to determine what you believe. I can bear witness to this reality. Many times in the past, I have witnessed people who gave up during their trial because they thought it was someone or something else.

The other deception is when you believe you have to go through the trial alone. I am serious when I say this—do not go through this alone! The belief that you do not need anyone else or that you do not want to bother other people with your problems is a lie! God's promises are always true. He will give you the people for your life who will walk with you. A good parent walks with a child going through difficulty instead of pulling them out of the situation because they know the child will gain wisdom from it for the future.

Unbelief

For a very long time, I referred to a small part of my person as "my little nugget" who had no eye for the present and glimpse into a future without Jesus. My little nugget knew what worked or thought she did. She caused me a great deal of unrest, fear, and anxiousness about the future. She refused to believe even though the rest of me had. She thought if she kept trying *her* way, things would work out. Many people have betrayed her, yet she used the same methods to feel needed and known. She made me anxious about the future by sowing seeds of doubt. If this sounds familiar, read on, and experience what the Lord told me about my little nugget.

"Little nugget, you have nothing to fear. You are safe and saved now. The Lord, your God, is here. I am all you need. You must see my love, and I tell you it is REAL! No earthly person will fill the void, only the love of your Father. No human will love you as you desire until you allow the Father to love you; until you love Him with all of your heart, soul, and might. Let down the armor around your heart. I want to heal your pain once and for all. There is no reason to resist. Little nugget, you remind me of a scared little girl. I just want to pull you into my arms and tell you everything will be okay. Rest now in the warmth of my presence. I will walk with you from now on. I will never leave you, never change, and will always desire to prosper you. I will show you how to love."

As a believer coping with unbelief, distrust, and doubt are primary methods the bully uses to keep you trapped. You love God, but when unbelief rises, the natural response is to retreat into your comfort zone even if you are curious. It is okay to have doubts. The disciples spent three years with Jesus, continually exchanging their misgivings for the reality of who He was and learning a new identity. Keep reading this book! Find a faith community where you can ask questions. Pray with an expectation of receiving more faith. Let God show you who he is. My hope is that as you continue reading, you will be able to see yourself through the eyes of Jesus, beautiful and with a significant purpose.

Unbelief and comfort can become your worst enemies. They deceive us into the belief that mediocrity is a good thing, with no need to take any real risk. This lukewarm place feels safe and comfortable. You can believe there is a God but just not for you. Staying in the middle lane seems like the best decision. On occasion, you can feel a stirring, but comfort's voice is pretty persuasive. It can be challenging to understand what is happening with your mind and soul when Jesus draws you closer. It is very natural to feel like you are conflicted with yourself. You may vacillate between the comfort of remaining the same in unbelief or taking a step of faith. I remember being in this place and wrestling with everything in my mind. God is powerful enough to cover your fear with His peace.

Self-willed

Are you stuck in survival mode and pridefully pat yourself on the back for "just getting by"? Oh, how the bully loves your scars and unhealed heart wounds. Survivors take pride in their battle scars. Are you striving forward, gritting your teeth, clenching your fists to survive? Do you solve problems as if you are putting out fires because you cannot get ahead? Do you feel powerless to move forward and wonder why you even bother?

If you are a self-willed person, complete surrender sounds very risky. For most of your life, you have relied on your own ability to survive and likely took pride in your battle scars. You assume an identity as a survivor. This is yet another great deception. The bully will even attempt to take advantage of your belief that you are in control. In the book of Jeremiah, this very popular verse states, "For I know the plans I have for you, says the Lord. They are to give you hope and a future." He is waiting. The sheer simplicity and uncertainty can be frightening. Letting go of everything you know as real—everything—and surrendering to a God you cannot see is undoubtedly frightening.

Our human best is continuously at odds with our holy best. You are incapable of fixing yourselves to the standard of your holy best. The holy best is possible, but only with God. Remember what you create; you have to sustain. What God creates, He sustains and invites you into. As the transformative power of grace begins to work within your life, you change much like a seed that begins to sprout. God's design for you is to know and trust Him, to discover freedom, abundance, and purpose.

Grace is the soil the seed is planted in. The soil has everything the seed needs to germinate, sprout, grow, and become what it is intended to be. To resist the work of our holy best causes great discomfort in our lives. It can cause unrest, strife, anxiousness, or even fear. Grace helps your heart understand what your head cannot. It is the message that trickles down into your spirit. My experiences of exerting my own will always seem like a good idea at first. It feels like freedom to be making my own choices as an adult and living my best life. Self-willed choices can seem very natural, but only for a short time until calamity or strife happen. The key point here is to recognize it for what it really is. You can turn the situation back to God at any time and seek His solution. Living a life as a follower of Christ means we mimic his lifestyle. In the context of this relationship, we submit, meaning we surrender our own thoughts, ideas, and plans to a superior plan; a surrendered heart and mind are the best defense against emotional manipulation and tactics of the bully. We become a seed under the utmost care of a perfect gardener.

Come out of hiding

There is a beautiful moment in Genesis right after Adam and Eve are awakened to good and evil knowledge after they ate the forbidden fruit. They cover up their bodies and hide from Him. The beautiful part is that God pursues them, and they come out of hiding. They are not left abandoned in this new state of being; instead, God shows them love and provides direction for their future. Nothing about the dynamics of this story has changed. God continues to pursue us not to punish but to redeem and restore. Testimony after testimony across the centuries reveals a Heavenly Father whose perfect love was displayed to believers when they came out of hiding. Most would share that they knew they really could not hide anyway.

As broken believers, you may think you cannot be restored because of the sin in your life. If you feel like you are being punished for falling away, stop for a moment and consider what a delicious lie and opportunity this is for the bully to keep his grip on you. Please know this is not true. Each day you wake up is another chance at restoration, peace, and real joy. Some people believe they have to hide from God when the truth of the matter is, He knows everything already. God is not mad at you, nor is He disappointed in your failures. He knows when you choose to live life on your own and are tempted or do not believe. Truth bomb—He loves you anyway!

The moment when you turned to Him and experienced His love was real. He knew your moment would come because He chose you. You are safe. Yes, even now. More than anything else, I want you to know there is a glorious life beyond where you stand today. The journey to this glorious life begins when you lay down your questions, doubts, and fears, hesitation, and stop seeking to fill the hole in your heart with other things. Stop taking the easy way out. It is killing you! Literally and figuratively, your resistance to God kills every chance for true peace, joy, and abundance. Living a life as a Christ-follower means we mimic his lifestyle. In this relationship, we submit our thoughts, ideas, and plans to a superior plan; a surrendered heart and life are significantly less likely to be tempted.

Discussion~Journal~Activation

In which ways do you identify or relate with the description of a broken believer?

In which ways have you previously not pursued your faith journey?

Do you understand that God is not mad or disappointed in your past decisions?

What did you learn about the soul by reading this chapter?

What was your understanding of the bully before reading this chapter?

Knowing now that God *chose you,* and you no longer have to hide from Him, practice your new identity as you go throughout your week. Journal your new practices and share them with a friend.

Chapter Two

The Gift of Completeness

The Lord is my Shepherd; I lack NOTHING.

Psalms 23:1

Ashley's story

Ashley is the epitome of a modern-day woman. She is independent, healthy, and living entirely for herself. She moves throughout her days centered on her own interests and bends the rules to fulfill them. It would seem to everyone around her that she has it all together. Yet, in the early morning hours, she lies awake next to a man who is not her husband and comforts herself with the stories she makes up about their "relationship." Lying there trapped, not strong enough to get up, to resist the fix of temporary attention or what it buys. Every aspect of her life seemed to be under her control until it wasn't. Recently her friends started to pull away or not include her in outings; she was passed over for a promotion.

The deceptive voice in her head fires up to say she is not good enough. Seeking after temporal things like high rise condos, fine food, and luxury cars make her feel powerful. The reel repeats the lie in her mind that she is unfixable, and because of her past, is incapable of believing she could ever live like that. "Like that," you know, valued for her unique talents and abilities, receiving healthy love from her husband, family, and extended circle. Then comes a still small voice whispering the hope of a one-eighty lifestyle. It allows her, if only for a moment, to dream of what life could be like if she could get past the hurt, clean up her life, and make her way back to Jesus.

Ashley's story is a parallel interpretation of Gomer from Hosea's book in the Old Testament. This account is heard from God's voice to Hosea to inform him what will happen to Gomer. It illustrates Gomer's inner world—a common ground for broken believers. There are times when you can no longer sustain the life you create, and everything seems to be crumbling around you. Any effort you put forth to create success, as you have always known it, fails.

The Bible refers to Gomer as promiscuous; she has a way of satisfying her soul needs by obtaining unsavory relationships, fine foods, wool, linen, olive oil, and drink. By standard cultural references, this Old Testament character would be known as a prostitute. While researching this chapter, I discovered a challenging definition that could broaden or even change your perspective. This definition that really struck me is the "unworthy or corrupt use of one's talents for the sake of personal or financial gain." Wow! Immediately, I reflected on all the times I used my talent to bend the rules for personal gain. I looked to a future absent of God's grace and made an inferior choice. I imagine we have all done the same. I am not accusing broken believers of prostitution but rather making a point of comparison to the inner world of someone who deeply desires a better way but could be trying to accomplish it in their own strength.

In the Bible, God tells her husband that God is drawing her into thirsty places to turn up the whisper of hope and speak tenderly about how He sees her. It may seem like her life is falling apart. When in reality, God is attempting to redirect her all for the purpose of growing her into the person He originally created. It is quite natural to resist what sounds too good to be true and settle for what we can accomplish in our own strength. In your own strength, achievement is limited to your talents and in subjection to the world and the voice of the bully. What God wants for Gomer, and by comparison, you also, is to lead you into a place where He can tell you how exceptional and loved you are.

Throughout the rest of Hosea chapter two, God tells Hosea how He will draw Gomer into the wilderness so He can speak to her tenderly. While it is true that Hosea's marriage becomes a living example of how the Israelites strayed from God, the illustration can be brought down to a personal level. God goes on to tell Hosea that God will take away her grain and new wine. He will stop all of her celebrations and expose her lovers, along with a list of self-willed actions and behaviors. Let me be clear here, it may seem like punishment at first, but like a loving father, God disciplines those He loves. Notice he is not dropping a shame bomb on her. The drawing away is for her benefit. The whisper of hope is to edify her and draw her nearer to God, the father, who wants so much better for her. His ways often contradict the conventions of society. However, He can use our circumstances or even common parental discipline tactics to discipline us.

Have you ever found yourself in a timeout? I know it is an often-used method for disciplining children, but I think the principle applies to God as well. A spiritual timeout is a season when God tries to get your attention to draw you near. It can be mistaken as a failure when it really is a divine set-up. You can go willingly or with whichever level of discomfort you choose. Timeouts look like the absence of people, places, and things from your present. Think about the comparison to Ashely's story. She suddenly cannot succeed in any area of her life. What if God is trying to get your attention and you futilely attempt to replicate the same behaviors with current or new jobs, people, and places. Hosea 2:14 states from God's voice, "I will lead her into the wilderness and speak tenderly to her." God tells Hosea how He will change it from a time of trouble into a time of hope. Did you hear that? God wants to change your time of trouble into a time of hope.

Hosea 2:14-15 refers to the Valley of Achor as the valley of trouble. I would liken it to a modern-day timeout. God's promise from these two verses is His desire to change what has been a time of trouble into a time of hope. I wonder how many times you see a crisis or try to pray away the struggle when God intends to help you shed off negative people, places, and things to draw us into a deeper relationship of trust and intimacy with Him. In this place, you can learn who He is as a father, who deeply loves His children. Earthly relationships and pursuits that you create without God, you have to sustain, and they can lead to difficulty if your life is not submitted to God.

The opposite is also true. What you create with God, He sustains. Have you ever experienced times when things are going along nicely; suddenly, a shift occurs, and nothing works anymore? You can think that it is everything else, but God often orchestrates your circumstances. I believe we often resist the transformation God wants to do because we lack an understanding of His true nature. It is my goal for you to come to an accurate knowledge of God, one that dismisses comparison of earthly relationships or experiences. Spiritual timeout is unto something-part of growing and maturing so that you become a blessing to others.

Could God have immediately taken Gomer out of her infidelity and idolatry? Yes, but it is through our mess-ups that we become aware of our need for Him. We were not created to go solo in this life. In a spiritual time out, God is actually trying to reveal the gift of completeness to you. Remember, we can choose the level of discomfort in which we go into a spiritual timeout. In this story, and in real life, God is long-suffering for us. He is a God who gives warnings, which expose sin, yet does not shame. He offers a promise to remove bad habits and to re-establish Gomer's identity through Him. God shares with Hosea that because Gomer continues meeting her own needs and not acknowledging Him, God will "block her path with thornbushes; and I will wall her in so that she cannot find her way. She will chase after her lovers and not catch them."

Right about now is when this becomes personal. How many times have you known something was not right for you and continued to pursue it only to be unsatisfied or unfulfilled despite the obstacles? Have you pursued unhealthy relationships because you were lonely? Have you used substances to mask or dull pain? I wonder if, in looking back, you could see the mercy of God trying to block your path with thorn bushes.

Let me recap. Whether an Israelite nation or an individual person, God is portrayed as a loving father who wants to remove unsavory people, substances, and places from your life, your mind, and your heart. God, the loving father, will attempt to protect you from going into those places, even to the point of removing you from people, places, and things in your life, because He wants your undivided attention. There is no place in this story where shame or condemnation are mentioned; God Himself is speaking! Another example of a timeout is in Psalms 139:5, where David is recounting his own experience with the Lord by saying, "You hem me in behind and before and lay your hand upon me." How God deals with Gomer is an example of how God lays His hand upon you as a loving father. God's standard of a loving father pales in comparison to even the most attentive earthy father. I want you to begin to open your mind and heart to the possibility of this being a divine appointment. Consider for a moment that God brought you to this thirsty place to read this book because He has great plans for your future, to offer you the gift of completeness.

The Gift of Completeness

"It is finished." "Tetelesti." Of all the words Jesus spoke on Earth, this is the most significant, yet least understood. How could one word have so much power yet seemingly be hidden within the depths of our Bible? How could the King of Heaven suffer so much to offer us freedom and power, yet we passively sit by with an idle mindset? The heart knowledge of this one phrase can be the seed of a transformed life. Jesus died for every test and every trial you have faced and for those to come. Victory in each one is ours if we choose to believe. The inside scoop is that the Lord wants us to understand that when we are tested and stretched outside of our comfort zone, it is to grow in faith, power, and understanding of who Jesus truly is. We are drawn away from danger and into His presence where we are safe. We walk into the valley of the shadow, LACKING NOTHING. God wants to reveal HIS strength against the accuser. Holy dependency, opposite of any human reliance, is appropriate. As you mature in the Lord, you will learn that His Kingdom is often opposite from the world. Holy dependency on God creates strength, hope, peace, and joy.

The most challenging marathon to run is when the eighteen inches between your head and heart are not aligned. Head knowledge and heart knowledge are two entirely different understandings. Head knowledge is how your brain interprets reality. To your head knowledge—mind will and emotions—"it is finished" is never black and white. Our head knowledge immediately prompts us to ask many follow-up questions such as "Are you sure it is?" Or, "What do you mean by finished; is it done for now or permanently done?" Through concrete facts and other people's actions, the brain interprets an "either/or" reality when the higher truth is a "both/and."

Heart knowledge, on the other hand, is what your spirit understands without any visible evidence. It is like believing the sky is blue even if you are colorblind. Or, like knowing the Atlantic Ocean exists without having been there yourself. The marathon from your head to your heart has many treacherous obstacles that can make it difficult to receive the gift of completeness.

The phrase "It is finished" has significant meaning to the heart. In the Greek language it means "now all things have been finished that might be fulfilled" or "to bring something to completion." It was the last word Jesus spoke before he died.

Through Adam and Eve, sin entered the world, and man's sinful nature still exists in humanity today. For more than 2000 years, humanity strived—meaning forced through self-will—to create a reality that only God can provide. God loves you so much that God manifested Himself through Jesus Christ; Jesus came on assignment to overthrow sin's hold on us. Jesus lived for 33 years and only began his ministry during the last three years of his life on Earth. One of the first acts Jesus completed after being baptized was to be led by the Holy Spirit into the wilderness where the devil tempted him for 40 days. The most common teaching on this event is that Jesus was tempted in every way by satan, but I offer another perspective. I firmly believe this event was to serve satan an eviction notice. He did all of this because of His extravagant love for you.

He sought out the enemy to destroy his hold on your life. In just three short years, Jesus raised enough disciples to proliferate the church into modern-day, and all with His simple message of grace, freedom, and truth. "It is finished" means Jesus won the war against sin for humanity and allowed us to become a new creation. This extravagant gift is always complete, always available, and designed to return you to your original royalty position as a child of the Most High God.

The Passion Translation gives us this very powerful illustration from Colossians 2:14-15, "He canceled out every legal violation we had on our record and the old arrest warrant that stood to indict us. He erased it all—our sins, our stained soul—he deleted it all and they cannot be retrieved! Everything we once were in Adam has been placed onto his cross and nailed permanently there as a public display of cancellation. Then Jesus made a public spectacle of all the powers and principalities of darkness, stripping away from them every weapon and all their spiritual authority and power to accuse us. And by the power of the cross, Jesus led them around as prisoners in a procession of triumph. He was not their prisoner; they were his!

When you believe in Jesus, your heart knowledge increases your understanding of who He is and who you are in Him, and your head knowledge will follow. This is so key! As you commit your life to understand what "it is finished" truly means, it means we are ALREADY victorious over the grip of sin in our lives; we only need to receive it. Let me repeat that. You only need to trust that God cherishes you beyond compare. This gift empowers us to believe we no longer have to agree with the voice of accusation. He has already won the fight for each of us; we only need to accept and trust in His victory declared within that seemingly simple phrase. It is finished for Ashley, and it is finished for you.

Do you know how to take the first step toward LIVING a life that mirrors Jesus' sacrifice for YOU? Could it be that living a transformed life becomes possible—even probable—with a fresh perspective and new understanding that is only gained when you lay down your control and submit your life to God.

Testing, temptation, and trials can attack us from various sources. In every situation, what comes to you God will use to strengthen you. He can turn any situation into goodness for His glory when we receive the gift of completeness. In Ephesians 6, we put on the armor of God, not our personal armor. I want you to come to an understanding that you LACK NOTHING when you place your trust in the gift of completeness. God wants to reveal HIS strength through you, against the accuser.

Fighting can be second nature to some of us who would say we are survivors. Fighting for survival is how we have always succeeded.

What if fighting for survival, as you are so accustomed, is literally preventing you from everything you have deeply desired? We often think we have to exert our will in a situation to take control of it. We consistently strive to make our circumstances submit to our will. What if we could flip the script? How different would it be if we would simply agree Jesus has already won? Our role is to stand, pray, worship, and study and <u>live out</u> the Word. Time and again, the Bible tells us that God fights our battles for us. He does the heavy lifting, not us. Both human will and dark forces are inferior against God, who sustains and protects us with perfect love.

A broken believer's life becomes more peace-filled when they realize that the existence of evil is an inferior and defeated force. Based on inadequate human experiences, it can be difficult to conceive in human minds that a perfect father could offer perfect love through a perfect son. Yet, it is true! Even more difficult is to imagine the King of Heaven would come to Earth, as a man, to defeat darkness for <u>you</u>. There is no greater truth than this. He came for *you*. Nothing you have ever done could separate you from perfect love. NOTHING! This perfect love is a gift that cannot be earned, and this love is undoubtedly extraordinary! The book of 1 John tells us that God is love; everyone who loves has been born of God and knows God. It defines love as how he loved us and sent Jesus as an atoning sacrifice for our sins. We love because He first loved us. When we experience love, it is because the Creator first loved us.

Discussion~Journal

How have you viewed God prior to reading this chapter?

What do you currently perceive differently about yourself, your faith, and God?

How do you see yourself in Ashely's story?

Discuss or journal your thoughts about how God loves us. I give you permission to be 100 percent honest with yourself and others.

Activation:

Find a quiet place to be alone. It can be in your car, in a park, your favorite spot in your home. Set aside the expectations of what you think it is to pray. In this time, you can listen to worship music, read the Bible or devotional book, or write your thoughts in a journal. Intentionally allow God to have your undivided attention each day. Complete this activity for 7 days, and review what you have recorded on the eighth day. What conclusions did you draw?

Chapter Three

Divine Love

"You don't even have to call out the darkness in people, just the light and goodness. Everything else has been defeated, so why give it your attention. Love transforms way easier than religion; it confronts issues because they're killing you. Love wants you to live and live more abundantly."~ Kristin DeMarco

The perfect example

The perfect example of Divine Love in pursuit is how Jesus walked with the disciples during His ministry. All four gospel accounts reveal how twelve men, clinging to their history and their way of navigating life, are radically transformed in just three years. Far from perfect, even to the point of betrayal, they slowly realize Divine Love in action as Jesus teaches them how to love others as themselves. The disciples were overwhelmed with curiosity because His message provoked them, unlike anything they had heard. They consistently witnessed a teacher who demonstrated love in a radically different manner as He said, "love your neighbor as yourself."

In patience and longsuffering, Jesus taught the disciples the meaning of Divine Love. He represented God, the Father, who deeply loved each one. The message was quite simple. Love God first and most. Do not worship any other Gods. Over time, they let go of their history as they came together in a family-like community. In this community, they practiced loving each other and others the way He had taught. Jesus addressed with ultimate patience their insecurities, uncertainties, and even their betrayals. Only at the cross did they realize the depth of His love and that He came to overcome the grip of sin in their lives and give them eternal life. Nothing about this relationship dynamic has changed. Millions of people all over the world share this commonality in their faith journey. Jesus walks with us as we let go of our history to embrace Divine Love. It is a journey as unique as each one who reads this book. In our instantaneous culture, we have an expectation of "three easy steps to success." Embracing Divine Love is a life-long relationship, a lifelong journey in which we exchange our current reality for the perfection of God's love.

Of all of the many types of love, Agapao—Divine Love in action—is the most unique. Close in definition to Agape love, which means unconditional love from God, Agapao translated from Greek, is a verb that encompasses Divine Love <u>in action</u>. God imparts Agapao Love to a human soul when we respond with belief, to His many gifts. Agpaoa Love is a supernatural love only experienced in a relationship with God, where He gives you the gift of Himself. Therefore, Agapao is radically different and incomparable to even the most treasured human connection. This scripture from second Peter provides more depth to the fact that:

His divine power has given us everything we need for life and godliness through the knowledge of Him who called us by His glory and excellence. Through these, He has given us His precious and magnificent promises, so that through them you may become partakers of the divine nature, now that you have escaped the corruption in the world caused by evil desires.

Unlike our past experiences with various human relationships, where love is withheld or leveraged, He will not withhold from you. God's very nature is to impart His divine nature to all who desire Him. Divine Love does not require any acts of performance from you. In other words, there is no action you can take to "clean yourself up," for God loves you wholly, even at this very moment, in any confusion, denial, or uncertainty. The simplicity here is there is nothing you can do to alter it.; He already loves you, and you have to agree with it.

Love will not rest

The constant and continued pursuit of humanity plays out from Genesis to Revelation. God pursues Adam and Eve out in the garden not long after they have disobeyed Him. Throughout time there has always been the dichotomy of humanity drifting away, with God in pursuit. His message of hope and love shows up everywhere; John 3:16 shows up in sporting events, spray-painted on billboards and park benches. This simple lesson points out that God so loved the WORLD, meaning His loving-kindness is not limited to a specific group of people. He cannot love more or less. Just as faith is given in full measure at the point of salvation, God's Agape Love is also given in full measure; we receive in the measure we believe. There is an unending supply of His love; you can have as much as you desire. I think the Lord would want you to know He understands your past experience with unhealthy love. His desire is for Divine Love to become the foundation from which you measure all other relationships within your life. As you weigh the difference between your past exposure to human love and God's perfect love, let me remind you that you ARE worthy to receive this amazing love. I know—it sounds untrue, and yet you are drawn to the hope and curiosity of the idea. The still small voice inside you questions the possibility. Dare you take the chance? I encourage you to lay down everything people have said about you. Release every negative title placed on you by others, every negative thought you are currently believing about yourself, and exchange it for perfect love.

Agapao Love Motivates

The journey to seek God came at this pivotal moment in my life. Pridefully, I thought I had it all figured out until I did not. Prescribed to the world's definition of success, I was winning! My career was progressing, and my kids were happy and healthy. I lived in my dream home and married my college sweetheart. Never mind the scars and unhealed wounds I still carried from the past. I did not realize I needed God's love until my entire world turned upside down when my marriage fell apart. Nothing made sense anymore; in one moment, everything I thought was true became a lie. All of the insecurities of my unhealed wounds resurfaced to compound the pain I was experiencing. I went from a self-confident, strong woman to a broken, hurting, and insecure woman at the end of her rope. My circumstances seemed hopeless! In the first few days, I lived in the pit of despair, unable to do anything.

Conventional therapy was my first choice. I hold a bachelor's degree in psychology and counseling; therefore, it was the natural next step to help relieve my distress. Even today, I believe in the benefits of therapy. In my experience, therapy drew out the pain, identified it, gave it a name, and offered coping mechanisms. That's not healing! My expectation was far greater than learning how to cope with the past. I wanted my heart and mind to be made entirely new. It was only after discovering the limits of therapy that I decided to see what God could offer. In true fashion, God exceeded my expectations and has never disappointed me. He made my heart and mind new as I continue to pursue Him and understand the gift of completeness. Supernatural healing is personal and extraordinary, making it difficult to explain to someone who has not experienced it for themselves.

Let me attempt an explanation. We all have voids, empty places in our hearts we try to fill up with substances, people, or activities as a meager attempt to comfort the soul. The soul is mighty and can deceive us into justifying almost anything for the sake of filling our voids. While your spirit is redeemed when salvation comes, your soul is restored over time as your body is brought into submission of God's good and perfect will. God gives you His perfect Spirit and lavishes his many gifts upon you. Supernatural healing offers wholeness because of God's Holy Spirit, which lives inside you. No longer are we left to cope with the past on our own; the void gets filled with His Spirit. Over time, you will exchange your history for God's good and perfect will. This is a continual life-long exchange rather than a one-time destination.

The more you let loose of your grip and surrender, the more He fills your life with love, peace, joy, kindness, forgiveness, patience, faithfulness, gentleness, and self-control. History always tells a different story than any moment in time. Looking back, I can see His hand orchestrate all of the events in my healing. I can now see His constant pursuit of me my whole life. With all honesty, I can say that I hold no offense from the past. My expectations of complete healing were met; all the ravenous places in my soul that need constant replenishment are now everlastingly filled with the love of Christ.

Unhealthy love

As long as we are talking about love, the Bible has a great deal to say about love, so it should not be a surprise that we can define unhealthy love by what scripture says. 1 Corinthians 13: 4-6 confirms that love is not jealous, does not brag, is not arrogant, does not act unbecomingly; it does not seek its own, is not provoked, does not take into account a wrong suffered, and does not rejoice in unrighteousness. Do you notice the common denominator in these verses? Each example of unhealthy love points to "self first." I am going out on a limb here to suggest we have all experienced both sides of unhealthy love. I only bring it as a contrast to what God offers us with Agapao Love. A prideful soul is unwilling to let go of its own needs long enough to consider a greater love. Unhealthy love will not allow the higher standard of God's love to be the example for other human relationships. Be mindful of this comparison as you continue reading.

An example of unhealthy love could be a friendship in which friend one expects friend two to meet all of their emotional needs. The opposing dynamic is that the second friend's needs remain unmet, and they are not equipped to ask friend one for the reciprocity they deeply desire. A skewed view of "being there" for friend one, sacrificing self for the sake of friendship, becomes unhealthy because forsaking self is not shared by both friends. This example can be applied to more than just friendships. Broken believers pursue unhealthy relationships because they want their own needs met or believe sacrificial love will win the other person over. Remember, temptation comes dressed as everything you think you want. If any relationship becomes one-sided, it can quickly become unhealthy.

Therefore, healthy love develops when two people or a group are secure in their identity, grow together to create a healthy shared identity, and continually place others' needs before themselves. In doing so, love reciprocates healthy love. Do you see the similarity of a relationship with Jesus? Think back to the beginning of this chapter and the perfect example. Healthy love does mean that you love others as Jesus loves. There is much to be said about boundaries in relationships. I believe in them, but it does not have to be complicated. Time and again, humanity complicates this simple yet profound message of love. Healthy love rejoices with the truth; bears all things, believes all things, hopes all things, endures all things. It is essential to know the difference because broken believers are prone to accepting and settling for unhealthy love when God's design for you was healthy love. In later chapters, you will learn why settling for unhealthy love can be a deceptive set up from the bully.

Oh, don't trip on that

If I could throw up a caution flag, it would be here. Because we remain in enmity with the bully until Jesus comes to take us home, he will continuously try to step up his game. Be on the lookout for everyday temptations and accusations that have worked against you in the past. Many believers have jumped in with both feet only to be presented with temptation, doubt, or self-willed desire designed to keep them trapped. There is nothing new under the sun. Consequently, I assure you the bully's tactics are limited.

Remain alert to what is happening around you, especially when the "reset" button is pushed. Do not be surprised when the things you are trying to break free from come calling again. Be aware when an imitation of something you have long desired rings the doorbell. It is not complicated to pursue God's will for your life, but it will be difficult. Jesus says those who lose their life gain it. It is true and quite beautiful. At the same time, broken believers can be conflicted about "losing" their lives when the fear of the unknown seems so great. However, fear is a horrible storyteller. Fear sells you lies that your comfort zone is the best place to be. The greater truth is your comfort zone is far more dangerous than the unknown, especially with God. Like any other relationship, it is a process of learning about each other and growing in devotion.

I mentioned this before but let me repeat it. Maintaining your footing each day is a process, a lifelong relationship of exchanging our inferior realities with the truth of Heaven. God has already given us every possible tool to be successful. We have His Spirit as our teacher. In later chapters, you will learn about these. We grow equivalent to the degree by which we surrender our lives and devote ourselves to a relationship with Jesus. As time passes, a tipping point occurs; God's will for your life becomes the greatest priority. At this precipice, you realize that you want what He wants for you, instead of leaving Him at church on Sunday to go about life as usual.

The greater reality is you were created by Divine Love, to know Divine Love, be Divine Love, and reflect Divine Love to others. You will live with a deeper understanding of who you are and how the Father sees you. The more you seek to understand, the more your appetite for a transformed life will exponentially increase. I write this book so that your knowledge of Agapao Love will flourish and find its way to the deepest crevices of your heart. Secure in God's love for you and well-equipped; you will send the bully packing. My prayer for you is, as you read, you will experience Divine Love in action over your mind, heart, and circumstances.

Discussion~Journal~Activation

How have you experienced unhealthy love in the past?

How has your understanding of love shaped or limited your experience of God's love?

How does it feel to understand that God is pursuing you right now?

How has the bully tripped you up in the past?

You just pressed the reset button. Describe and journal about how you want your life to look.

Chapter Four

Your Journey Is Real

"The journey of a million miles starts by taking the first step." Lao-Tzu

Roger's Story

A dark-haired man sits crossed-legged on the floor of a hospital room. He is slumped or. His white hospital gown is oversized, but it really does not matter to him. In fact, judging from his body posture, he really does not care about much at all. A quick glance at his hospital chart tells me Roger is his first name. As he lifts his head to meet my gaze, I realize how he has bought the lie. I look straight into his eyes, and my heart sinks in disbelief. I know you are in there somewhere, Roger, but the eyes I see tell a torrid tale of an unjustly tormented soul. "He bought the lie," I say under my breath. I see a young boy longing for love but rejected by adults. He bought the lie that he wasn't important. This lie led to purchasing many other lies—lies that caused poor choices and wrong turns. Lies that resulted in addiction, complicated by sick love with a cocktail chaser of guilt and regret. If we were to look back into his family history, we would see just how children were treated.

Children are often not treated as cherished leaders of the future but as a burden to the parents. The orphan spirit rests on past generations sprinkled with jealousy, alienation, turmoil, and self-centeredness. The principles of "get it while you can" or "I live to make myself happy" have long been ingrained into the family DNA. Roger is a product of generations trying to succeed in life in their own strength, confused by the world's messages. With the odds stacked against them, they become survivors. The human will is so fascinating because it causes us to be persistent, often with ideas, people, places, and things that have a short shelf life. We persist in continuing to try only to discover our limitations. The result is feeling trapped.

    I sit down on the floor, facing him. I can see from looking in his eyes that he had been sedated. The tattoos on his forearms tell me the story of a young boy in the oversized shell of a man. Man, I remember that feeling! From the time I was very young until I received salvation, I experienced this sensation of walking around as a shell of a person much larger than who I really was, trying to prove to myself and the world I had it all together. As a child, it was frightening not to understand it. At night, I would lay awake feeling so small, afraid, and unprotected. The uncertainty in the circumstances around me only compounded how unprotected I felt. I made rules for myself as protection. Rules = walls that held me captive from healing. Then, I had no words to explain what I was experiencing. Now I understand that my body was an empty vessel without the Holy Spirit.

Healing your heart is not a "one and done" process; it takes time and commitment to the process. The first time we allow God to heal us is usually the most difficult. It could be that we lack heart knowledge of Him and, therefore, do not trust or have faith for healing. We may believe healing is for others. That in itself is a lie. Healing is also very personal and will look very different for each person. Reject the natural instinct to compare your healing to someone else's. I can offer you this wisdom; do not resist what God wants to do in your life. The closer you stay to the Father, the easier it is to receive healing and step into a NEW life.

Where you have been and what has happened to you matters

Throughout this book, you will find that I spend the majority of my focus on who Jesus is and who you are in Him and less time addressing your brokenness. For each person who reads this book, there will be a multitude of circumstances, singular, and plural, that have brought them to their knees. I have had the privilege to walk with many people who carry the weight of the past as they have walked with the Lord. Some have had multiple challenging experiences, while others get lost in a singular traumatic event. Some have suffered at the hands of friends or family, while non-family members or even strangers hurt others.

This chapter is not intended to be a deep dive. Instead, it is merely intended to fully acknowledge what happened, what brought you to this moment. Clarify in your mind the very reason you chose to read this book. God does not waste suffering. You are here in this very moment, divinely appointed to read this book. It is essential to validate what brought you here and to offer you a hefty dose of wisdom with the hope of moving into a beautiful future. For some, it may take more than wisdom. Pursue your healing with Jesus, and do not settle for anything less than complete healing.

It is vital to acknowledge where you have been and any traumatic event(s) in your life. In this chapter, we are going to touch on a few key points to work through. Consider this chapter, the crossroads. Visualize yourself there, standing at the crossroads of your past and future, with a dusty suitcase in your hand. This suitcase has been everywhere with you; it is where your disappointment, pain, fear, doubt, confusion, and shame hide. You open it, occasionally, to make sure your trauma was real. In many ways, the pain validates the trauma. It is human nature to be needed and known; innately, we desire our pain to be validated by others. Acknowledgment makes our offense and our feelings valid. The choice of sitting the suitcase down and stepping into a beautiful new future may seem simple to those who have not shared your experiences; they are your own. While any offense becomes part of your story, the danger is believing you have to live with the offense or let it define your present and future. Do not let it keep you from experiencing the life God designed for you. The dusty suitcase, while well-worn, separates you from freedom. As a broken believer, it is imperative to understand the circumstances around the last time you fell away as you work through this chapter. What gets exposed to the light can be healed, and what stays in the darkness will continue to cause separation.

It is very natural to question where God was when you experienced trauma or why he did not prevent the trauma from happening. The answer is not a new one. We live in a fallen, sin-filled world, which means bad things happen to good people. To be honest, I struggle to use that answer because it seems like it is not enough for someone who has experienced trauma, myself included. I can tell you what God told me when I questioned Him about the one instance of abuse I suffered. He explained how He was never invited to heal others' brokenness, so they repeated a cycle. Jesus told me, "my heart grieves because I was not invited in. It was my heart's cry for you to know me when you were a child. Instead, I waited all of those years of your life to be invited in." WOW!

God will never force himself or his ways on anyone even though He profoundly desires to. This single encounter explained so much! No one in my family—for generations—knew they could invite God into their broken places, which leads to healing for them and following generations. As a result of this encounter, I begin to pray and ask God to bring healing into my past and present areas. In prayer, I invited Him into my family. I fully expect to see changes. You can do the same. Simply say this prayer with all hope and belief in your heart:

Father, I invite you into every broken place in my life. I invite you to heal every broken place in my family, where hurt and trauma has carried on for generations. You are the only one who can create new life from darkness. Through Jesus, healing and restoration will happen.

In Jesus' name, I pray, Amen.

Please understand that you cannot put a band-aid on the deep wound of unforgiveness. Forgiveness is a choice, one that does not deny the offense but instead empowers you to move forward with divine strength, peace, and the hope of a much brighter future. The reverse is also true. Harboring unforgiveness can perpetuate bitterness. Bitterness can have a plethora of adverse emotional, mental, and physical side effects. If you have caused pain in someone else's life, you can receive forgiveness too. In fact, forgiveness is never about the other person. The true nature of forgiveness is to help <u>you</u> overcome and heal. Quite frankly, any measure of forgiveness you can extend to yourself or receive from another person pales in comparison to the forgiveness God extends to us so freely and abundantly.

As you work through this chapter, my hope is for you to set down the dusty suitcase and step into a beautiful new future. I intentionally left the word offense as a vague description because there are so many ways to become offended. You are thinking of your offense right now. Something you have held onto for a very long time. In 2 Samuel 22:20, David is recounting how God delivered him from the hands of ALL his enemies and Saul, "You brought me out into a spacious place; you rescued me because you delight in me." God wants to bring you into a spacious place because He delights in you. Cling to His promises, and know that He holds onto you more than you cling to Him. Will you let him? He wants to set you free from the personal offense you've experienced; it cannot be hidden because He knows and sees all. So as you read about the three ways people harbor unforgiveness, take time to acknowledge the past, how you carry unforgiveness, how you hold onto it, and let Jesus take it from you. You might want to gather a few close friends who will listen and support you.

Bury it

The best way to explain this is to use me as an example. I buried my dusty suitcase of unforgiveness in the backyard of my soul. Each time a new offense occurred, my response was to dismiss it, never realizing I was not free from all the previous offenses. I would continuously retrieve the dusty suitcase to add more stuff to it. I was working against myself because to dismiss the current offense meant I had to open up a suitcase of past offenses.

Contained in every lie is some element of truth; it is why we believe lies. The lie I harbored was that I was supposed to turn the other cheek and not let the past bother me, and in doing so, I would be okay. You can only do this for so long before it begins to affect your behavior. The dusty suitcase becomes a burden we were never meant to carry. I was given the identity of a "strong person" very early in life. At first, in my teens, I thought this was a compliment. I adopted the identity for myself, falsely believing I could never be vulnerable to others because it would blow my cover as a "strong person." I exchanged the truth for an inferior reality. Now, I understand what was hidden from me then. Burying it was not releasing it. Let me say that again for the people in the back row. Concealing it is not releasing it.

Imagine the impact of someone with years or even decades of burying their feelings and past trauma. Wounds of any kind without healing continue to compound in your life. Everything buried weighs you down physically, emotionally, and mentally. Unforgiveness unhealed will manifest in different ways. It can become the worst game of Whack-A-Mole you ever play. When you bring your wounds into the light and expose it to the supernatural healing of Jesus, He will also heal the hidden hurts within the darkness of your soul.

Beat ourselves up

When you mess up, you will have to stop choosing to enter the room of regret while picking up the past mistakes to inflict pain upon yourself. Beating yourself up about the past is one of the most common tactics the enemy uses to keep broken believers from receiving healing and walking in wholeness. The lie is that your past mistakes are so terrible, you are not worthy of a transformed life. The voice in your head sounds like, "You did [fill in the blank]. How terrible! How could you ever be worthy of a life unburdened from the past?" You will have to become so uncomfortable with the lie, deeply desiring a new truth—the real truth! There is always an opportunity for exchanging the lie for God's truth. It begins by closing the door on the room of regret to seek after God's will with the understanding that His will for you is always good.

Blame others

This one is a bit touchy so let's be clear. Anyone who has unjustly committed an offense against you is wrong even if they were never exposed. The difference is what you decide to do with it—blaming places power in the offender's court, often without them even knowing it. The related emotional pain can deceive us into believing we are judge and jury against them. As broken believers, we have to adopt an eternal mindset; the wrath we carry for the offender can become a burden getting in the way of how God wants to heal your heart. From beginning to end, God's word is very clear about this for both the broken believer and the offender. You are a child of God, highly cherished. Exodus 14:14 tells us that "The Lord will fight for you, while you keep silent." Throughout scripture, God fights for His people as a righteous defender. Your choice is surrendering the blame to a God who says, "Whoever conceals his transgressions will not prosper, but he who confesses and forsakes them will obtain mercy." Proverbs 28:13

Let God deal with them righteously while you press into the healing that Jesus sacrificed Himself to give you. The God revealed in the

Bible is a God capable of sustaining his people and keeping them faithful irrespective of how severe their difficulties or how pressured their lives. He is incapable of being unfaithful. Will you trust him?

Healing the past, present, and future

Hopefully, by now, you are beginning to get a picture of who you are in the eyes of Jesus and how much He loves you. Now it is time to step out of the shadows and into the light. The band-aid will no longer be enough to cover up your pain. The beautiful healing light of Christ will guide you, in partnership with the Holy Spirit, to become who you were meant to be all along. As accurate as this statement is, it will not seem beautiful at times, and for some of you, this is not your first time being here. In fact, a large majority of this message is intended for broken believers who have tried to fight in their own strength and have failed.

When failure sets up camp within your mind, you decide to throw a party and invite some friends such as shame, fear, and confusion.

Receiving Christ means that you received full redemption. In Christ, everything the enemy stole is restored to you. If you lose relationships, God promises to never leave you and to give you the people for your life. Every small victory builds on the next one, like a domino effect that heals the past, present, and future. What you allow God to heal in your dusty suitcase and not carry forward actually has a multiplying effect on your future. When shame is healed, it makes room for holy assurance to rest in your heart. With holy assurance in your heart, you make better choices. Better choices result in better future outcomes. The more healing you receive, the more divine strength you receive, which transforms your future trajectory. For the rest of this chapter, you will begin to gain insight into the common tactics used to keep you trapped. Buckle up, Buttercup, it is about to get real!

Do not accept the invitation to the plain of Ono

In the Old Testament, the book of Nehemiah of his personal encounter as a cupbearer to a Persian King. Nehemiah hears that his people are in danger and disgrace, and in a divine moment, he gets permission and full resources from the King to rebuild their wall so the Jewish people can have protection around their city. He arrives to assess the city walls, and as we read in chapter two, he meets opposition from a group of men who question his assignment and authority. From that point on, as the story goes, this group of men continually try to thwart Nehemiah's plans even to the point of inviting him to the plain of Ono.

I want to draw a parallel here to your journey. Nehemiah's enemies attempted multiple times to stop him from accomplishing his divine assignment. The word of wisdom here is that as you progress into a deeper relationship with Jesus, you will have to leave some people where they are. It does not mean you completely cut them off. Love them where they are, share what God is doing and invite them to come along. Keep moving. Growth often means your interests are different than theirs now, and the temptation to go back into the plain of Ono is real. Like Nehemiah, who had too much at stake to get drawn away, you need to reject the invitation back into environments that have historically pulled you away from God in favor of a far greater future.

Nehemiah was laser-focused on his assignment; he was all about what God wanted to do through him. He also understood the risk of entertaining conversation with the enemy. It was not about the people trying to pull him away; they were merely pawns. It was a set-up for Nehemiah to be drawn away from completing his assignment. Once you push the reset button on your faith journey back to God and into a relationship with Jesus, the bully is going to attempt to draw you away, much like Nehemiah. Remember, it is not about the people. It's about the potential of a set-up to be drawn away from God. .Armed with this new insight, you will be alert to his tactics in the future. There is never a hit like the one you do not see coming. With this fortified awareness as you read each chapter, you will be equipped to resist and succeed just like Nehemiah.

The windshield is way bigger than the rearview mirror

Years ago, I was at a restaurant, having dinner with a friend. I arrived a few minutes early, which is quite unlike me. I am usually a few minutes late everywhere I go. I asked the hostess to seat me while I waited for my friend, and she agreed. From the moment my friend arrived and throughout the meal, she complained about her ex-husband, who had divorced five years prior. Five years!! I would try to offer her encouragement, but that was only fuel for the fire. There was no dialogue or reciprocity in what was happening in my life because she was so hyper-focused on her divorce five years ago.

Finally, after two hours, I looked her straight in the eyes and said, "There is a reason the windshield is bigger than the rearview mirror." I explained that as long as she continued to dig up the bones of the past and drag them into the present, she would be looking through the rearview mirror, which has the warning on it. *OBJECTS IN MIRROR ARE CLOSER THAN THEY APPEAR*. I explained that her choice was to lay the past to rest and embrace the windshield view of life. I encouraged her to focus on where she was going and not where she had been. Complaining is the language of the person who feels powerless to change. The lesson here is there are choices to be made every day. You can choose to buy the lies of an inferior reality or exchange them for the gift of completeness, which contains everything you need for real transformation. The windshield perspective has a much clearer view of your options. How you perceive your world is really in your control.

Do not buy the lie

Thoughts or actions that are set against the knowledge and character of God and your beautiful identity in Christ is a lie. Any act of temptation, confusion, unbelief, or distraction is a lie. As Christ-followers, we make choices of which voice to listen to and focus on. Will you agree with the voice that speaks hope, peace, and joy or the voice of mediocrity?

The inferior voice may sound off in your mind with thoughts that your faith-reset button is broken. The voice sounds something like, "You tried, and it didn't work, so it must not be for me." Agreeing with this thought creates a domino effect of other defeating thoughts that will keep you trapped. The best lie is the one that sounds most like the truth and mirrors your current reality.

Another common thought, rooted in stubbornness, might say something like, "if God is so powerful and loves me so much, let Him come to me." The shroud of stubbornness prevents you from seeing that He already did! The gift of completeness exists for all who will receive it. If you see yourself in this lie, go back to Chapter Two and review the depth of the gift of completeness. Repeat after me. I will not buy into the lie. It might sound humorous now, but it happens all the time. Broken believers buy into a lie and trade God's truth for the lie.

Remember, the best lie is the one that sounds most like the truth. When a lie is purchased, the bargain is never an even one. We always get short-handed, exchanging something of higher value for an inferior product. You are often exchanging peace, hope, joy, or love for an insult. The lie of "you are not worthy" is exchanged for the perfect love of a Heavenly Father who calls you His Beloved.

I want you to begin to develop a keen awareness of how this exchange happens in your mind. As these scenarios arise, intentionally stamp them "RETURN TO SENDER." Remind the sender that he already lost and that you are highly favored by the King. Remind yourself that this time is different because you are equipped with the protection of God's power, and *you will succeed*. No longer will you clip coupons to buy lies. There will be no more buy one lie; get one for free. When you develop a "full price" mindset, you choose to believe what Heaven says about you, always in humility to what Jesus did for you. "Full price" rejects the lie in favor of your full identity in Christ.

Serve the eviction notice

The accuser comes to steal your joy, kill your hope, and destroy your mindset. Remember I explained in Chapter Two that Jesus sets an example for us to serve the bully an eviction notice? This declaration was the ultimate act of intimidation, one that Jesus followed through on with His death, resurrection, and ascension into Heaven. Sin no longer has a grip on you! Jesus did all of this because of His extravagant love for you. He sought out the enemy to destroy his hold on your life. While we will have enmity with satan, he lacks the power to be anything other than a bully.

You are no longer a victim. No longer do you have to allow life to happen to you. Instead, declare your freedom over the bully.

You have the power to send the bully back to hell, where he belongs! These comments may seem like humorous satire when I am quite serious. Consider the facts that Jesus came to give us freedom from the bonds of sin—inferiority, to show the perfect love of the Father, and to give us eternal life. The flesh, the world, and the devil are already defeated for YOU to live abundantly beyond all measure. Your response is to evict the bully and embrace the full price mindset.

Discussion~Journal~Activation

Where have you harbored unforgiveness in your life? Take time to work through this. Allow the Holy Spirit to show you where those places are. You can journal or discuss them with your tribe.

What lies have you bought?

What are you willing to exchange the lies for?

Are you willing to embrace the "full price" mindset?

Are you looking through the "windshield" or the "rearview mirror?"

What have you kept within your dusty suitcase?

Do you now have a clearer understanding that healing in our own strength has limitations, while the healing God offers is to fully restore and make new?

Spend time practicing this "full price" mindset. Journal or discuss what you learn.

Chapter Five

Grabbing hold of the future

"In Him, you have redemption through His blood, the forgiveness of sin, in accordance with the riches of God's grace which He lavishes on you with all wisdom and understanding." Ephesians 1:7

A personal interpretation of Psalms 23

From the mountain top, the valley is lush and green. The air is so fresh and clean. The smell of pine permeates the air. My eye catches the snow-capped peaks covered with clouds of white and the palest ice blue. The coolness in the air reminds me that a fire will be necessary this evening. I am surrounded by the details of natural beauty, yet; I cannot escape the fact that I came here to do business with the Lord—to partner with Him. My armor makes a clunking sound as I descend into the valley flanked on my right by Goodness. He is a mighty warrior who walks with the most fantastic sense of integrity. His strength is righteousness. When he speaks to me, it is as if the Lord is nourishing my soul. On my left, Mercy shows me compassion. She reminds me, in her majestic warrior splendor, it is okay to make mistakes. I do not have to be perfect because the Lord is. The sun is bright in the sky, and it casts shadows from one ridge to the other. I set up camp near the foot of the mountain—nothing fancy here, just my armor, backpack, tent, and sleeping bag. However, sparse, I know I'm not alone, with Goodness and Mercy nearby.

I am here on assignment; of this, it is clear. I will come face to face with my enemy who accuses me night and day. He thinks I am afraid, but he does not understand I have been in training. I have studied my opponent and understand his tactics are always the same.

This covert mission will not last long because my King has already worked out the victory. You see, the accuser's biggest weakness is arrogance. He gets way too much credit for the tactics he employs when, in reality, he only has limited power. The mission is to defeat him and overthrow his stronghold on my destiny.

The shadows grow longer. It does not take long to set up my tent and sleeping bag. I am surprised by how comfortable it seems to my aging body. Mercy and Goodness assure me everything will be okay. They encourage me to go and walk with the Lord down by the stream. I see Him in the distance waiting for me, and as I approach Him, he takes my hand. We walk along the mountain stream. I find it difficult to take my eyes off of Him. Every time I make eye contact, it is as though I can see the whole world in His eyes.

"You know I love you, as does the Father. You are so pleasing in our sight. This battle is for you, but not about you." "Yes, Lord," I say as my spirit comes alive. "We believe you are strong enough to overcome it. You must use the gifts you were given to overcome. You lack nothing, for I am with you always and will never forsake you."

Nightfall is coming soon, and as I walk back to camp, I collect dead limbs for the fire. Hmmm? Dead limbs are nature's way of pruning. Pruning reminds me of how the Lord has removed unhealthy branches from my life. Habits and mindsets that kept me from wholeness and my royal identity. As I bend down to collect the limbs, I recount what they represent; lust, poverty, pride, shame, and an orphan. Yes, reminders of training and how sweet it will be to watch these dead limbs burn and become heat and light. The Father wastes nothing. The mindsets broken off me will one day allow me to speak the truth to another's life. For now, I focus on my assignment. Back at camp, Goodness and Mercy have already started a fire, and much to my surprise prepared a meal. Mercy tells me I will need my strength tomorrow, for the Lord will do amazing things among us.

The fire crackles with a beautiful orange, red glow. We began to worship God for all He has done and all He will do. The dead limbs of the past are cast into the fire. Goodness and Mercy rejoice with me as I dance before my God. Much to my surprise, God comes near to hear us. His presence is so strong, yet so beautiful. We can sense His delight. Suddenly, angels appear, and the sound of their worship is unlike anything I have ever heard. Pure joy! Pure sound! My humanity does not have the vocabulary to describe the perfection of their worship. In fact, in the presence of God and angels, I want for nothing. I am entirely unaware of my physical body or any desire or need. Goodness comes to my side, suggests I sleep now, and leads me to my tent. I drift off to sleep with the lullaby of angels worshipping God.

In this creative narrative that parallels Psalms 23, the writer recounts her training and grabs hold of her future. How did she arrive at this beautiful place? Why is she so confident? You, my dear, are about to find out.

FAITH + GRACE = FREEDOM

What is faith? *Faith is the assurance of what we hope for and the certainty of what we do not see—rooted* in the belief of times, things, or events that have yet to happen. You believed one day you would be married, graduate from college, or travel. When your belief began for any of these events, there was likely no guarantee it would happen, yet you believed anyway. A baby taking its first steps believes in the impossible. Establishing your belief in something sets it in motion. The difference between belief and faith can be fuzzy until you stop to consider which one is first. Believing something will happen is the first step to embracing the faith for it. The human will is capable of incredible feats once it genuinely believes. Remember when I explained about heart knowledge and head knowledge? Belief begins in the heart. However, it is not without some neurological underpinnings. A significant amount of research has been conducted within the past twenty years around the idea of belief related to spirituality. I love learning how intricately God created us! One conclusion of this research is our minds are created with cognitive biases to believe in the unseen and supernatural. I would suggest being made in the image of God produces a holy discontent to discover "something better."

So, it is within our thoughts that the beliefs sprout. Perhaps our minds send a "green light" signal to our hearts. Romans 10:10 states that it is with your heart that you believe. In the same verse, the Passion Translation says, *"The heart that believes in Him receives the gift of the righteousness of God, and then the mouth confesses, resulting in salvation. For the Scriptures encourage with these words, "Everyone who believes in Him will never be disappointed."*

Having tackled belief, what then is faith? It is the unwavering hope-filled belief that God is good and His plans for you are also good. Faith carries our hopes into reality and becomes the things we long for. It is all the evidence required to prove what is still unseen. It is a mindset that understands, to the core, that God loves you perfectly and deeply desires abundance for you. Faith agrees with what Heaven has already decreed. The question then becomes will you receive it? Faith + Grace = Freedom.

When you believe or establish your faith, God lavishes his gifts of grace on you. Grace is explained in much complexity by many authors, teachers, and scholars. Simply put, for this illustration, grace is a supernatural gift that allows you to leave your dusty suitcase at the crossroads and step into a new future without ignoring the past or being shackled by it. We all have fallen short; notice this past tense. It goes against the character of God, who relentlessly pursues His children to give them good and perfect gifts they cannot repay. Therefore, grace is a gift, a mindset that sets you up for understanding your identity in Christ. God wants you to know that you are worthy! He created humanity in His image, full of meaning and purpose. Through Jesus, grace becomes the vessel in which God transfers His righteousness to you. God did not create us to be the sum of our mistakes. Grace shields you so you can grow and receive the gift of completeness.

When you believe that Jesus died for the sin of the world and to overcome death, you are regarded as a new creation. As part of His gift of grace, God restores you to the original state once you believe in Jesus' sacrifice. Our old nature, the desire to have and be what the world wants, fades away. God begins to strengthen you with His desires—His plan and purpose for each of you. Laws and rules provide a moral code, but His grace covers you. We have direct access to God as he invites you into a relationship with Jesus. It is the transforming nature of this relationship that changes you.

Receiving grace is as much a physical experience as it is a spiritual one. With a shifted heart, you move throughout your world differently. You see life through an alternate lens. You become sensitive to people, places, and things that used to not bother you. You somehow understand that you are loved and protected by God. His grace begins to fill a void in your heart before you even realize that's what's happening. Faith + Grace = Freedom. You become free of the world's standards and begin to experience God's standards.

We, humanity, are made by Him, and in His image, with the desire for relationship. God designed you with a desire to know him and to be reconciled to Him—to return home. What other God would create such an intricate design and desire to be in a relationship with you? This is not a one-way God! This is the God who created you before the world was ever formed. He knew you as you grew in your mother's womb; He numbered the hairs on your head. He gave you a purpose and a calling. He loved you before you were you. The desire you have to be needed and known came from Him. The beauty you see around you, He created. The order of nature is His design and His power.

The gift of grace is God's design. From Jesus' sacrifice on the cross, the act of absolution gives each believer the gift of unfathomable grace. Grace is the inherent gift that keeps on giving. God's grace covers you, restores you, and changes you. It is a divine setup designed by your Creator to make you holy and blameless before Him, through Jesus, who came to earth as a man. Jesus experienced every part of man's sinful nature, so you might have a high prince who can empathize with our weakness and intercede on our behalf. Hebrews 4:15 says that you can now freely enter into God's presence with the confidence he intended for you to have. Holy confidence holds no comparison to self-confidence. Holy confidence is who you are in Christ, not who you are on your own. Grace gives you the space to develop holy confidence. Faith + Grace = Freedom.

Grace fills in the gaps

Honestly, I thought that grace was this ethereal thing that separates me from sin—as in "covered by grace"—but for a very long time, as a new Christian, I never put all of the pieces together. While you can agree on the ethereal definition of grace, I would suggest that grace is tangible and plural. Grace gifts are lavished on you when you believe. Remember, the gifts of salvation, faith, and grace are given to you in full measure. As your soul begins to believe, faith in God grows, and your love for Him increases. You will begin to learn about yourself like never before.

I want to be clear about something. God does not call His children to be perfect. Grace fills in the gaps. It takes time to create a lifestyle that is submitted to God's will. Can He instantly change your circumstances this instant? Absolutely! What you miss out on in the process strengthens you and helps you understand God's heart toward you. In the process, grace fills in the gaps. Grace covers you from the grip of shame, doubt, and fear to keep you moving forward—into your destiny. It is a gift you can do nothing to obtain. God has already determined you are worthy of it. Grace fills in the gaps as you learn and grow in your faith.

This transformation process is truly a lifelong journey, taking two steps forward and one back, making mistakes. Please hear me; you cannot continuously pull the grace card when you repeatedly and willfully pursue wrong choices. Grace holds our place in line, so to speak, so you do not have to start over. If you allow it, God will use your mistakes to teach you how to do better next time. Each time you learn what success looks like, you will better understand who you are and how God loves you. Grace will give you the power to resist temptation. No one is perfect, and what you did in the past cannot keep you from a beautiful future. As you have already learned in past chapters, you are no longer held guilty in the courtroom of life, your dusty suitcase is back at the crossroads, you have stopped buying the lies, and you have evicted the enemy. You, my love, are well on your way to becoming who God initially created you to be.

Faith, plus grace, equals freedom. Your belief and faith in Jesus Christ, plus the grace God gifts you, will create the key for you to be free.

Awaken the gift

Humanity was created to be in a uniquely intricate relationship with God. Instead, we fill our hearts and minds with other things. Absent of this beautiful relationship, you chase after people, places, and ideas. We listen to the voice of the world that tells us to fix ourselves, try harder, earn more. We are judged by our outward appearances and achievements, all the while internally having angst of unfulfillment—

a God-sized hole in our hearts. God wants to release seeds of hope that will grow deep roots and release his Kingdom purpose into the earth.

Redemption from sin is the first gift, and most people are satisfied to stop there. I ask you, when have you known God to stop there? Look around you, all of the detail in creation, all the complex intricacies in humanity. Would a God who created so much detail be satisfied with the only redemption for his children? Do you not have a duty to pursue Him so that you can discover what He has just for you? You have a heavenly promise that when you walk in grace and obedience, you will be blessed coming and going. The passions, giftings, and talents you have are evidence of God's purpose in your lives, even when you do not acknowledge Him. Each one of you is uniquely, fearfully, and wonderfully made according to Psalms 139. Only when you spend time sitting before our Maker, actively listening, can you

FULLY develop these passions, giftings, and talents into divine purpose.

Will it be easy? You know first-hand, from past experiences, that it will not be easy. I hope that with a greater understanding of who God is, spiritual confidence in who you are to Him, plus a fortified arsenal and toolkit, success will be yours. By His divine pleasure and marvelous grace, your gifts are confirmed before the foundation of the world.

God's word is living and can be deeply meaningful to you right now, and can be recounted through Paul's writing form 2 Timothy 8-10:

For God has not given us a spirit of timidity, but of power and love and discipline. Therefore, do not be ashamed of the testimony of our Lord or of me His prisoner, but join with [me] in suffering for the gospel according to the power of God, who has saved us and called us with a holy calling, not according to our works, but according to His own purpose and grace which was granted us in Christ Jesus from all eternity.

Your gifts are CONFIRMED! You already carry our holy calling. I have said it before, but what God has portioned for your life cannot be taken from you. God is not like that. He is drawing you into Himself to open your mind and heart up to what He has already given. Embrace your position as a Child of God and all the power attached to this royal identity. Your gifts are always there, waiting for you to arrive at an understanding of this truth. Your spiritual gifts await your willingness to go into training.

Your mission, if you choose to accept it, is twofold. First, accept and receive all that God has already prepared for you. If you have read this far, you know that abundance of salvation, freedom from sin and death, gifts of faith, grace, and purpose await you. You may also begin to understand why the bully would not want you to understand the truth. What if the bully, the world, and your own understanding have held you back from everything God has portioned to you simply by deceit? What if everything God has portioned for you is on the other side of deception? Right about now, a holy discontent should be rising up to say "no more!" Therefore, fan the flame of these gifts you have been given by spending time developing a relationship with God through prayer, reading the Bible, and worship. Secondly, build up your holy confidence and begin to steward what God has already given you with the help of the Holy Spirit.

My heart desires that everyone who reads this will move from being broken believers to mighty warriors of God. I pray you develop a laser focus on your relationship with Jesus, to chase after heavenly purpose. Imagine if a whole generation of broken believers lives a faith legacy that creates a cultural shift away from divisiveness, self-hatred, and self-willed desires to one of harmony, abundance, and unity!

Discussion~Journal

Have you ever considered how intricate God's design is? In the next week, notice the details of His design and make a note of them in your journal.

Do you accept this mission? If so, what excites you the most? What scares you the most?

What beliefs do you need to let go of to receive the abundance God has for you?

How has your understanding of grace changed?

Did you understand your gifts already existed? Do you have any clues to what they could be?

Ask God to speak to you as you spend time alone, writing out responses to these questions.

Chapter Six

The Helper

Frequency

Every living being that has life has an energy, and therefore, has a frequency. Frequency—typically measured in waves—is defined as the rate at which something occurs or is repeated over a particular period of time. Sound and light are two common forms of energy that are measured by frequency. Resonance frequency describes the condition in which an electric circuit or device produces the largest possible response to an applied oscillating signal. The word resonance originates from the Latin word resonare, which can mean to resound or echo. Through resonance, a comparatively weak vibration in one object can cause a strong pulse within another. An object free to vibrate tends to do so at a specific rate called the object's natural, or resonant, frequency. This resonant frequency depends on the size, shape, and composition of the object. Such an entity will strongly vibrate when subjected to vibrations or regular impulses at a frequency equal to or very close to its natural frequency. By analogy, the term resonance is also used to describe the phenomenon by which an oscillating electric current is strengthened by an electric signal of a specific frequency.

Let's break this down a little more. I am suggesting the Spirit of God has a resonance frequency. The human being is made of the body, soul, and spirit. Our soul reigns over our mind, will, and emotions. Our spirit is what connects us to God and the heavenly realms. Think back to that unique and moving moment when you felt God's presence. Let your brain remember the moment as your soul recounts how you felt. Then recall what you touched, heard, smelled, saw, or felt. This sensation was Heaven coming down to connect you and awaken you with the Holy Spirit. What a glorious moment it was! You were drawn into the presence of God and became fully alive with the resonance frequency of Heaven through the Holy Spirit. Maybe it felt like electricity flowing through your body. The presence of God came near you, and because He is life, he is also energy and therefore frequency. He resonates a frequency to your spirit, supernaturally speaking to you. The frequency of Heaven cries out to be heard. You were made in the image of God to experience God's presence through the Holy Spirit.

There is no reason to shy away from or fear the Holy Spirit. You may not be familiar with God's presence, or you may have experienced it without understanding what it is. Either is okay. The disciples did not understand it either. They wanted Jesus to remain on Earth to continue teaching them, but Jesus had another assignment. He explains to the disciples in John 14 that the Holy Spirit will come by saying to them:

If you love me, you will keep my commandments. And I will ask the Father, and He will give you another Helper, to be with you forever, even the spirit of truth, whom the world cannot receive, because it neither sees him nor knows him. You know him, for he dwells with you and will be in you.

Jesus goes on to inform them in advance that the Holy Spirit was their promise and future teacher.

These things I have spoken to you while I am still with you. But the Helper, the Holy Spirit, whom the Father will send in my name, he will teach you all things and bring to your remembrance all that I have said to you. Peace I leave with you; my peace I give to you. Not as the world gives do I give to you. Let not your hearts be troubled, neither let them be afraid.

The disciples needed a heavenly teacher to guide them. Nothing has changed; all believers need the power and tutelage of the Holy Spirit. This is yet another gift from a loving father who wants His kids to have a personal trainer. He knows the way and wants the best of everything for you. Time and time again, throughout the Bible, God promises His people He will never leave or forsake them. His spirit is the Holy Spirit, the same voice from Heaven guiding believers. The Holy Spirit has a big job, including bringing us the truth of God's word and ways, prompting you to respond. He also convicts us of sin.

If Jesus were alive today, His message to us about the Holy Spirit might have sounded like this: "When I leave, I promise to tie this all together. I am sending you what the Father promised—another helper. Wholeness is what

He will give you and not as the world gives. The world cannot give you wholeness. It can only come through the Holy Spirit. Do not let your hearts be stirred up. Stand still in my wholeness." You see, we are meant to have the Holy Spirit as part of God's plan for our wholeness.

One big moment

I have often wondered if unawareness of the Holy Spirit is the one common denominator missing from all broken believers. As I have pondered it over the years, I genuinely believe it is. For with the power of the Holy Spirit, we overcome with love, joy, peace, patience, kindness, goodness, faithfulness, gentleness, and self-control. I carry this belief because of my own before-and-after experience. I had a unique supernatural experience at salvation. I was chasing after God by reading the Bible and listening to everything I could get my hands on. In October 2011, I drove about three hours away to watch my kids perform in a marching band competition. To pass the time, I listened to a CD of a pastor preaching on several topics when suddenly and without warning, my whole being—mind, heart, and soul—were overtaken by the sensation of love like I had never known. This was perfect love, as it gently flashed the story of my life before my very eyes, reminding me that Jesus had been with me my entire life. I wept from a place deep inside, tears of pure joy and peace. Somehow, I never lost control of the car.

That experience remains powerful and unique to me today. It marked the beginning of an entirely different life for me. Over the next few years, my love for God grew. As I practiced my renewed faith, my understanding of God's word grew. I checked all the boxes by devouring God's word and serving in my church and community. However, I still had strongholds in my life that kept me from experiencing wholeness with God. I knew I was redeemed but could not overcome lust. My soul, wanting to be needed and known, chose less than ideal "relationships." I was still trying to wrap my mind around Godly dating contrasted with the world's standards. My assumption was I had to overcome these strongholds in my own strength. I was far too embarrassed to share my struggles with anyone within my church family. Do you see the trap? I thought I had to overcome on my own, and because I unknowingly listened to the wrong voice, I was trapped! But God already had a solution planned.

In 2016, through a small group experience, I gained new knowledge of God as my Father. I had to open my dusty suitcase and expose it to the light and love of Jesus. This small group activated a tipping point in my faith journey. Yes, I heard God's voice almost from the beginning as I journaled and studied the Word. The difference before is I left Him in my prayer closet and went about my day subjected to the struggles of my humanity. I love God and knew He was leading me to experience more of Him. As I continue to crave more of His reality and no longer wanted to unintentionally place human limitations on God's plans for me, I was awakened to the Holy Spirit's presence already dwelling inside me. God, through His Holy Spirit, dwells inside me! This realization completely blew my mind! When I tell you that you are worthy of this extravagant love, I am speaking from experience. God found you worthy at salvation to give you with part of Himself, all the while knowing you would mess up, doubt and struggle. He knew we would need a helper. Since then, I have an inner power that is not my own, to stand up to the bully, resist temptation and not buy any lies. This can be your game-changing moment like it was for me. The gift of the Helper is for you also.

Back to my question—what if lack of understanding of the Holy Spirit is the thing that keeps you stuck? What would it look like if an entire generation of broken believers realized the power of the Holy Spirit? No longer would we have to be trapped in silence and trying to save ourselves! Equipped with the knowledge of God's love, living out their faith in a relationship with Jesus, and being taught by the Holy Spirit, generations of believers could break free from satan's vicious cycle. The deceived do not know they are deceived—what a travesty! I might even go as far as to ask, would it not be characteristic of the bully to keep believers trapped in deception and personal sufferings? What if the bully feared the power and unity an entire generation of equipped believers could have on the world if they only knew about and began to desire the Holy Spirit? Are you stirred up? I certainly hope so. This book aims to help you gain strategies and new knowledge that will equip you for success in your faith journey. I will not undermine the other weapons listed in Chapter

7; they are essential. Nor do you only need the Holy Spirit. Both are essential. Equipped with both, you can live a transformed, purposeful life full of God's peace and purpose.

I imagine thousands upon thousands of broken believers walking in wholeness with God, full of Holy Spirit power and knowledge of God's Word. Romans 16:20 says, "The God of peace will soon crush Satan under your feet." I say a generation of believers full of the power of God's Spirit will soon crush the bully under our feet! Do you agree?

What you need to know

Through my testimony, you learned how the Holy Spirit is the inner power from God who withholds no good thing from His children. You have also learned His gifts of faith and love are given in full measure. When you receive salvation, the resonance frequency of the Holy

Spirit touches your spirit. In other words, you already have it. Since we receive in the measure to which we believe, all you have to do is pray for it to be revealed to you. It is the heart of your Heavenly Father to give you himself. In doing so, He can have a deeper relationship with you. Jesus teaches, "If you then, who are evil, know how to give good gifts to your children, how much more will the heavenly Father give the Holy Spirit to those who ask him!" Jesus gives a strong comparison, but he never minced words. It is a promise! Ask to be awakened to the presence of the Holy Spirit already dwelling inside. Keep praying specifically for more power to live a Christ-filled life and watch what happens in your life. Initially, you will notice a shift in your priorities. I stopped trying to fulfill heavenly promises with earthly methods. With the Holy Spirit as my personal trainer, I really began to take new spiritual ground. I started pursuing a lifestyle that was pleasing to God. Today, I am a testimony of God's love, Jesus' sacrifice, and the power of the Holy Spirit. Like me, you may have simply lacked the knowledge of the Holy Spirit. My hope is that your life is about to change for the very best.

For this reason, I bow my knees before the Father, from whom every family in Heaven and on Earth derives its name. I ask that out of the riches of His glory, He may strengthen you with power—through His Spirit—in your inner being, so that Christ may dwell in your hearts through faith. Then you, being rooted and grounded in love, will have power, together with all the saints, to comprehend the length and width and height and depth of the love of Christ, and to know this love that surpasses knowledge, that you may be filled with all the fullness of God. Ephesians 3:14-16

Discussion~Journal~Activation

What have you known about the Holy Spirit?

Share or journal your thoughts about the Holy Spirit's role as teacher and tour guide?

Ask God to awaken the presence of the Holy Spirit inside you.

Ask God to give you a vision for what your life will look like in one year. Write down the first thoughts, images, or impressions that come to your mind.

Close your eyes and imaging being part of a generation of believers full of the Holy Spirit. Record what you see.

Chapter Seven

Weapons of a Warrior

Casting Crowns, a contemporary Christian rock band, recorded "Slow Fade" in 2007. It is a message of caution of how what we do, see, hear, and think can impact our future. I would add that you may not even be aware of a "slow fade" in your life because it is so subtle.

"It's a slow fade when you give yourself away.

It's a slow fade when black and white are turned to gray.

And thoughts invade, choices are made, a price will be paid.

When you give yourself away.

People never crumble in a day."

Think back to the circumstances that tripped you up last time and how the slow fade drew you away. Were you fully armed? Did you know your enemy's tactics? Upon reflection, you may begin to notice the absence of weapons; remember, the weapons we fight with are not the same as those the world battles with. A warrior's weapons are prevention strategies, mindsets, and actions anyone can take to stand firm against the accuser who comes to steal, kill, and destroy. God brought you to this book because it is part of your journey back to Him. This time, you will be equipped to resist and stand firm in your identity.

There is no hit like the one you do not see coming

Know thine enemy and thine self. The primary defense mechanism used since the beginning of time is to know your enemy, understand the capabilities, characteristics, motives, and tactics as well as know yourself. Military leaders all over the world dedicate significant time and money to this primary defense mechanism. It plays out in sports too. The wise coach will study the opposing team's game videos to learn their moves and understand his team's abilities. You also can pull this well-known strategy down to the granular level to apply it to your own life. The slow fade often happens because we lack the knowledge and resources to fight. Well, that is about to change. In this chapter, you will discover the weapons of a warrior, strategies for protecting the new life you are creating with Jesus.

I think it is important to recap here. As warriors in training, we have an enemy, and he comes to steal, kill, and destroy. We also know Jesus already defeated him. Your salvation and destiny *cannot* be taken away by satan; he can, however, create confusion, distraction, and temptation. Deception is the basis for all warfare. Everyone has a part to play in discerning their actions and must take responsibility for them rather than automatically counting it as spiritual warfare. As your discernment grows, you will be able to tell the difference. The caution will always be to not give power to the enemy where he does not have it. We provide a subtle power shift to satan when we automatically blame him for an event when, in reality, it may be our actions or natural circumstances. We must avoid transferring authority for him to meddle and deceive. Our responsibility is to develop discernment so that we can recognize this. Now, let's begin the training.

The Bible confirms you do not have to reach a particular point of spiritual maturity to access the Holy Spirit, and when you believe, God grants His Spirit in equal proportion to all. The difference is how much you access it. God's

Spirit is our living water, our abundance without measure. By His design, our faith cannot rest on God's Word alone. Humanity has been known to take for granted or misinterpret the Bible. Only through the supernatural combination of God's Spirit living inside you can His Word truly come alive in your heart. Paul says in Romans 16 that when you study, pray and worship, the truth is revealed. As our relationship grows with Jesus, our faith muscles develop. When our faith grows, the transformation begins, and seeds of purpose buried inside you start to sprout.

The armor of God is a defensive weapon, while the Bible is an offensive weapon. Defensive weapons protect you from an enemy, while offensive weapons are used to attack or advance an enemy. We are gifted with both. Putting on God's armor is to shield us from influences that may try to control thoughts and behaviors; it is a protective measure to equip us to take our thoughts of temptation captive for Christ. Over time, this protection gives space to a new reality and a new identity. This new space allows us to fight offensively with the Word. The Word becomes flesh and dwells in you, giving way to holy confidence where you once struggled with self-confidence.

The mindset of a warrior

God is good

The fundamental starting place might seem a bit obvious; however, it bears repeating. The goodness of God, or shall I say, your understanding of the goodness of God, will shield you. When life goes wrong, and circumstances look bleak, your first line of defense is to filter your knowledge of God's true nature and character. Throughout the Bible, God reveals his goodness, even to those who do not put their trust in him. We see God protecting, guiding, defending, and showing favor. It is not true because it is in the Bible; it is in the Bible because it is true. The entire book—66 chapters—recount personal experiences and encounters where God's goodness is put on display. His goodness is displayed in nature's intricate design, the birth of a newborn child, or through the person moved by compassion. Shift your focus away from conflict or pain and to the goodness of God. Allow God to show you His goodness; this mindset is the foundation for all the other weapons' success.

Divine Love is at the center of the goodness of God. In John 1:4, we read that "In Him was life, and that life was the light of men. The Greek word light actually means Zo'e' fullness of physical and spiritual existence. If you go back to Genesis 1:4, we see God creating the separation of light from the darkness. In Revelation 1:9, where John tells us again, Jesus was in the beginning, and he is coming back for us. At the starting point was the conclusion, the final message. Jesus made all things, and separately from him, nothing was made. Everything God does is personal and out of divine love, including sending Jesus to Earth. In Jesus, is physical and spiritual life imparted to us to overcome darkness. I point out that Jesus was light in Genesis, John, and Revelation to demonstrate God's intricate design and goodness. He was thinking about you as He created the world.

Embracing Sonship

Sonship is the relationship between a father and child. It is not limited to a father-son dynamic. The analogy of this father and child dynamic consists of three parts. First is the Father, who is God, loving, and perfect in every way. He is also powerful and mighty. Second is the child who, being made in the father's image, carries all the same rights and privileges. Thirdly is the relationship. When this relationship is intimate, the child's identity is strengthened by the father and the child flourishes in life. When the connection is distant or strained, the child struggles. I offer this brief explanation of sonship because it mirrors a believer's relationship with God.

Broken believers often have difficulty embracing sonship because of past experiences with earthly fathers or mothers. Our heavenly Father often gets a bad rap even when He has done nothing wrong. Adopting the mindset that God's goodness is constant will help you embrace sonship. It will help you arrive at a new spiritual reality of what God did for you. Sonship has been expressed to you throughout this book in the theme of God's goodness. Sonship exchanges your self-confidence for holy confidence and understands your identity as a child of God who is lavished with gifts of salvation, faith, grace, and Divine Love.

Accepting sonship is the same as exchanging your inferior reality for what Heaven already says about you.

In Psalms 16:5-11, David gives the perfect exhortation of sonship. David was a man after God's own heart and knew God intimately. Here are his words from The Passion Translation:

Lord, I have chosen you alone as my inheritance.
You are my prize, my pleasure, and my portion.
I leave my destiny and its timing in your hands.
Your pleasant path leads me to pleasant places.
I'm overwhelmed by the privileges
that come with following you,
for you have given me the best!
The way you counsel and correct me makes me praise you more,

for your whispers in the night give me wisdom,
showing me what to do next.
Because you are close to me and always available,
my confidence will never be shaken,
for I experience your wrap-around presence every moment.
My heart and soul explode with joy—full of glory!
Even my body will rest confident and secure.
For you will not abandon me to the realm of death, nor will you allow your Holy One to experience corruption.
For you bring me a continual revelation of resurrection life, the path to the bliss that brings me face-to-face with you.

David expresses that blissful sonship is available to all who desire it; it is not reserved for the elect. In fact, Jesus taught against those who saw themselves as elect, for they were not humble enough to receive the truth. He makes a powerful statement that is necessary to understand, to embrace sonship. He states in Matthew 10:38, "Whoever finds his life will lose it, and whoever loses his life will find it." Embracing sonship begins with the understanding that you were not created for the limitation of this world. Instead, you were created by a Heavenly Father who wants to overwhelm you with the privileges of following Him.

Weapons of a warrior

Prayer & Worship

In previous chapters, you have learned how lies come into our thoughts and the importance of exchanging them for Heaven's reality. It is a lie that one must be at a particular level of spiritual maturity to pray or possess a unique ability to pray or that one cannot pray the "right" way. The greater truth is prayer is a private conversation with God. Jesus modeled this by going away from the crowds and his disciples to pray. He teaches us from Matthew 6:6, *But as for you, when you pray, go into your inner room, close your door, and pray to your Father who is in secret; and your Father who sees what is done in secret will reward you.* Nothing in this verse says prayer has to look or sound a certain way. It is a conversation with God, and He has already factored in any awkwardness you make feel.

Each time you pray, even in awkwardness, is considered obedience. God loves an obedient heart! Submitting to God in prayer becomes an offering. Recall the end of Matthew 6:6. God will see what you have done in secret and will reward you. Kingdom rewards manifest in many ways. I can remember, as a new believer, the first time God answered one of my prayers. My reward was the privilege to see God move and the heart knowledge to understand how powerful prayer really is. Over the years, I have witnessed God miraculously intervene in many ways, both small and large. Prayer is a practice of obedience and an accessible weapon for every believer!

When we become new, God's Spirit awakens inside us. Prayer opens your heart and mind to hear from God; it is like food for our spirit. Through prayer, the Holy Spirit shifts our understanding to see things from God's point of view and pray according to His will. Prayer is transforming, and the beginning is often the most challenging part. Here is a simple five-step method that I learned, to help you forge a habit of prayer:

Praise—Praise acknowledges God's true nature and character and His place in your life. It momentarily rejects our circumstances and turns our attention to God. Praise Him in advance of the fulfillment of a promise and acknowledge what He has done in the past and what you are trusting Him for in the future.

Thankfulness—Thankfulness reminds our spirit that God is the giver of all life, who brings peace into every believer's heart. Through thankfulness, your heart becomes yielded, contented, and grateful through the work of the Holy Spirit.

Confession/Repentance—Confession and repentance—the next section has more detail—are given to God for any sin in your life or unbelief in our minds. There is no condemnation here; it is a conversation with God. You exchange any lie for the truth of Jesus' sacrifice for your transformed life.

Bring your petition—Bring the plea of your own needs and the needs of all, including unbelievers, into the presence of God; some may know their needs while others may not. The Bible teaches us the Spirit himself intercedes for us with groans that words cannot express. Give room for what may seem unnatural at first and allow the Holy Spirit to describe your needs even if you do not know.

Intersession—Finally, we make time in prayer to pray for other believers and the place where the Spirit intercedes for all saints according to the will of God. Do not be surprised if your prayer for other believers changes as you continue praying.

As your comfort level increases, you will notice these five parts might be out of order, or some might get left out. It is okay! God accepted our human condition long ago. He is most interested in the posture of your heart toward Him first and others second. Even if it is small at first, the dedication you make to prayer will grow over time, as a unique foundation to your relationship. God loves bold, specific prayers that go beyond human ability. He likes to show you His goodness.

Worship is an offering of sacrifice to the Lord. Much like praise and thanksgiving, you extol God for who He is. In the Greek language, worship means "step forward to kiss." It is much more than singing along with songs at church or in your car. It is a response to God, who has reached out to love us. In worship, we come before God believing that He exists and that He rewards those who earnestly seek Him. He often rewards us with thoughts, impressions, feelings, and understanding of who God is and who we are in Christ. Worship is intended to be a supernatural experience. It is in this place that we give ourselves over in trust and surrender to His love. We ultimately know love because He first loved us, and while this is an offering to God, the results will benefit us. True, wholehearted worship changes us from the inside out. Essentially, God steps forward to kiss you and imparts his nature and character to you, often sharing Kingdom secrets with you. This is the spiritual intersection of head and heart knowledge. We should enter worship expecting to be different than when we came in. Such a sacrifice is always rewarded because God is incapable of denying Himself to us.

Repentance & Confession

Any unconfessed sin in your life can become a deception that creates an open door for falling away. It could be "the thing" that tripped you up last time. Our human nature resists repentance: just ask a child to admit they did something wrong when caught in the middle stealing a toy or writing on their dog with lipstick. It is not in our human nature to admit we did something wrong. If you have experienced a past traumatic event in which you were shamed or became fearful, you are even less likely to desire confession.

Selfishness, shame & pride are roots of unconfessed sin. Broken believers may resist because they bought the lie that their sin is unforgivable, their way is better, or that confession will bring harm. As broken believers, you may have done something that perpetuated or created sin in your lives. You either did not know what to do, felt shame because of it, or willingly pursued your own way. From this moment, separation from God began. One foot of separation became two hundred feet, which became two miles. You may have tried to pray or even go to church; however, you simply are powerless from any real change without confession and repentance. In a one-eighty lifestyle, repentance and confession are weapons. To know repentance as a weapon, you must understand what it truly is and is not. Let us start with what repentance is not.

Repentance and confession are not condemnation. If anyone is in Christ, the Holy Spirit is in them, and they are not condemned.

Condemnation shouts, "Your past! Your sins! You loser!" Sounds like a bully, does it not? Condemnation shouts while conviction whispers. Condemnation's goal is to spew shame, hold you down or pull you back into an inferior reality. The bully uses this voice to remind you of how you failed. You may think it is your thoughts causing a self-critical inner voice, but it comes from satan and is meant to tear you down. The greatest deception plays out when broken believers mistakenly believe God tells them negative or condemning thoughts. It is a bald-faced lie! Jesus said He came not to condemn the world, but to save it (John 12:47; 3:17).

Another common misunderstanding in this area is when we assign human emotions to a Heavenly Father. Contrary to popular belief, God is not angry at or disappointed in you. If you have learned anything by reading this book, I hope it is a deeper understanding of who God is. Assigning human emotions to God for falling away or messing up would limit God to human action and eliminate His supernatural nature to redeem, restore, and heal.

The opposite of condemnation is conviction. The inner voice of conviction is the work of the Holy Spirit within us to convince us of God's truth. It moves to build us up. When I talk about reading the Bible and learning the TRUTH, it is the Holy Spirit that teaches and allows the Word to penetrate deep into your spirit to convince and cause you to change the direction you were walking in. Conviction is a yellow caution light when you are heading in the wrong direction. Not only is God willing to forgive your sins, but He deeply desires to do so! Isaiah 30:18 says, "Therefore the LORD longs to be gracious to you; He waits on high to have compassion on you. For the LORD is a God of justice; How blessed are all those who long for Him." Also, "If we confess our sins, he is faithful and just to forgive us our sins, and to cleanse us from ALL unrighteousness." (1 John 1:9)

Repentance is admitting to God you heard the voice of conviction and are turning from your sin and toward God. The work of the Holy Spirit given to us by God redirects us back into a loving relationship with the Father. In advance of our transgressions, God creates a pathway back to Him through confession, repentance, and work of the Holy Spirit, who is the only force strong enough to bring conviction and put to death the misdeeds of the body. (Romans, 8:13). Through the submission of the Holy Spirit and in prayer, you are re-turning—turning again—or returning to the Father.

I want to clear up the unrealistic expectation of living a one-eighty lifestyle. Throw your expectations out the window because holding on to them will either limit you or hinder a relationship with God. It takes time to change because our human spirit and soul must continually come into submission and be trained in righteousness. Through the Holy Spirit, we overcome negative imaginations, self-destructive thoughts, attitudes, and mindsets that want to disprove God's truth, accuracy, and promises. The heart of the matter is that no matter what you are currently experiencing, the Holy Spirit will use the Word of Truth to change your circumstances for the better. As disciples, you submit your life to a holy God who, through His Spirit, re-programs your spirit and soul. Could God supernaturally impart everything you need to know instantly? Yes! But how, then, would you develop a relationship? As a warrior, we must daily train, gain knowledge, and build a relationship with God.

Solitude

One practice I can point to over the years that has made the most difference is intentionally setting a time each day to commune with God. After all, it is a relationship that requires spending time together. This space of solitude is where most of my training has taken place. It is where God gave me this message for you. These daily moments of solitude are where I have learned everything I am sharing in this book. Solitude competes with a very fast-paced culture that demands instant results; I think God understands this. As you begin training for the 180 lifestyle, set aside your expectations and do not compare your faith journey with others, for it is as unique as your thumbprint. If you commit fifteen minutes every day, that is a great start. If all you have is your commute time to work, use it to pray and listen to an audio version of the Bible. God will use whatever you give. Ask God what He wants you to know today and be open-minded about receiving His answer. Seek Him first in all things and watch what He will do.

Remember this part of your defense. It is where you go into training; the secret place is a strong tower—a place of refuge and strength. Psalms 91 gives a great example of how solitude is a weapon. The writer recounts personal experience of practicing solitude. It is here God speaks an intimate message of care and protection. Countless times when I felt anxious or restless and did not really understand why, I entered the secret place, and my joy or peace was restored. Communing with God simply means you have a dedicated place and time to meet. There is no fancy ceremony to perform thanks to Jesus. It is just you, God, and the Holy Spirit. It is in THIS place you can hear God speak to you. It is in THIS place, as you read the Bible that your head knowledge of God will transition to heart knowledge; you gain revelation you did not previously have, and, in intimacy with Him, learn what your unique giftings are. In this place, you will be trained and conditioned as a warrior of God and able to resist the accuser.

Though you live in this world, you do not fight as the world fights, which is completely counterintuitive to any other training. Use God's mighty weapons to knock down the strongholds of human reasoning and destroy false arguments that remain unsuspecting to those who do not know God or are not in Christ. In solitude, believers learn their identity in Christ. Here we are able to build up holy confidence and be strengthened to reject the lies of the flesh, the world, and the bully. Every obstacle of pride sets itself against the gift of completeness, against everything that already belongs to you as a child of God. Now, you can begin to see how solitude is a weapon. In this private place, you practice most of the other weapons.

Community

Community will look different for everyone. Some groups will only be two or three people, while others might be part of a larger group. Here is another area where expectation should be left out. We can become conditioned to think "church" is the only choice, the same way we become conditioned to believe big box stores are the only place to shop. You get to decide where you participate and what works best for you or your family. In this section, I want to give you a few words of wisdom when making your choice.

Find a community that suits your personality and be led by the Holy Spirit to discover the right place. It can be a bit of trial and error at first. Look for a place you can grow into, a place where others are growing and where peace rests. Peace is a fruit of the Spirit and should be present among other believers.

Peace will resonate within you as a witness to your spirit.

We are created to be social beings. If recent quarantine measures during a global pandemic have taught us anything, it is the deep-seated desire to be in community with others. For broken believers, being in a community of other Christ-followers can be uncomfortable. It is normal to struggle a bit to find your place in any social setting; this one is no different. I get it. However, a community can be a weapon or line of defense against the bully. The writer of Hebrews tells us not to neglect meeting together, and in early chapters of the book of Acts, they were together continuously.

The fruit of the Spirit marks real community outlined to us in Galatians 5:23-26. There is always room for questions, inaccuracy, correction, and growth. The community is also a place among other believers where your faith and spiritual gifts can develop and grow. Leaders are learning and growing just as much as followers. In fact, the ideal community will reject the formal definition of leadership in favor of a shared model in which all can and do lead from time to time.

A community is also a place of two "abilities," vulnerability and accountability. As your relationships develop in a group, others will begin to invest and take an interest in your life. Over time, as the relationship develops and your fellow group members learn about you, they can help you if a temptation or trial arises. Shared vulnerability and accountability is what the apostles and disciples were doing in the book of Acts. They grew in love for each other to the point of submission. They moved together in one accord, praying for each other. Their agreement is how God sent angels to bust Peter out of prison. Can you imagine having the kind of people in your life who would pray for you like this, who would really do life with you?.

Finally, a community allows you to see God move through other believers' lives, which is one of my favorite perks. Someone might share how Jesus healed them while someone else may share what the Holy Spirit taught them. The point here is we need the community of others to share and receive encouragement. Through prayer, repentance, and solitude, what you learn in the secret place can be shared and practiced in a community.

I firmly believe if you practice the mindsets and weapons of a warrior, you will not fall away again. In fact, I *know* you will not. Your success is guaranteed because of who God is. The mindset of a warrior understands their royal identity and embraces His goodness. You now know what to do to defend yourself in advance of a potential threat. Through prayer, worship, repentance, solitude, and community, you will become well-equipped to succeed in your faith journey. The only thing left to do now is to begin.

Discussion~Journal~Activation

How did your expectation of weapons shift from the beginning to the end of the chapter?

How did your expectation differ from what you read?

What mental blocks did you have before reading this chapter?

What was your mindset about God? How would you like that to change, starting today?

What weapons—not listed in this chapter—have you used to "fight" the bully or other people?

Activation: For the next 30 days, write your prayers in a journal.

Chapter Eight

The Prayer of Permission

"So now the case is closed. There remains no accusing voice of condemnation against those who are joined in the life union with Jesus, the Anointed One." Romans 8:1 The Passion Translation

You have arrived at the end of the book. If I have done my work, you have been challenged and have a fresh perspective for your faith journey. My prayer was for you to enter this book as a broken believer and leave a mighty warrior of God. You now know your blind spots or temptations that may try to take you down in the future. Healing from the past is not only necessary but a reality that awaits you. Remember, as followers of Christ, conflict, and confusion come when we try to fit an inferior reality into the context of God's superior truth. The gift of completeness is one that will continually give as you grow in faith and trust. The more you surrender your soul to this gift of completeness, the more you become who you were always supposed to be. You are no longer deceived into believing you are powerless. Instead, you are powerful to evict the enemy from your life and be part of a generation of revivalists.

Although God could have instantly changed your situation, I hope you now understand He would rather you know His heart and walk in a relationship with you as He strengthens and sustains you more each day. God creates a stirring, holy discontent to prompt our desire to know His heart for your benefit. This stirring beckons us to create margin in time for the Holy Spirit to show you God's truth. This is a drawing into a place of intimacy we would not otherwise experience. In this place, nothing is out of reach. Plant yourself in the grace and solitude of a trustworthy Father who's love will utterly transform you. So then, we must tune into what God is doing. Trust not only in your ability to hold on to Him but instead trust His ability to hold onto you. TRUST in His provision. TRUST in His character. TRUST in His promises. If we focus on the situation or circumstance, it becomes a distraction to the eternal Big Picture.

Pull back and see the bigger picture. God has so much more in store for you than you can imagine! Focus on the positive in your life and pray for wisdom. This reminds me of John 21 when Jesus stands on the shore and calls to the disciples, who have unsuccessfully spent the night fishing. He tells them to cast their nets on the other side. At first, they did not even recognize it was Jesus. They said, "No." A second time, Jesus, still unknown to them, tells them to cast their nets on the boat's right side. They end up catching 153 fish; one version says, "without breaking their nets." When Peter realizes it is Jesus, he jumps in the water and swims to the shore. The other disciples follow. When they reach the shore, Jesus already has a fire and meal prepared for them. IF they had dismissed Him from the shore, they would have missed the blessing. Jesus already had a blessing prepared for them. How often do we neglect the opportunity to partner with God because we are so focused on what we see and not on God's big picture? How often we pray away the refinement Jesus is trying to do in us, mistaking the trial as a struggle. God's plan for your life is so incredible! He will not set you up for failure. Every experience is unto something greater in His Kingdom.

Co-laboring with God is one of the greatest blessings we can experience. Beloved, the Lord is calling you to partner with Him right now, to bring blessing to others. Maybe it is something small, or perhaps it is something big. Look up and see that He is holding onto you, calling you closer to Him for the purpose of blessing. Ours is not a one-sided God! The blessing is always double-sided. He blesses you with more understanding of who He is, and you become part of the physical manifestation of blessing others. Each one of His children is a masterpiece, a re-created treasure that will fulfill the destiny He has given each of us, for we are joined to Jesus, the Anointed One. Even before you were born, God planned your destiny and the good works you would do to fulfill it. We become His poetry. How beautiful! The question now really comes down to what will you do next? If this book has done its full work, you will not be the same person as when you began to read. You will be compelled to act.

Discussion~Journal~Activation

Will you pray this prayer of permission?

Lord, give me eyes to see what you are doing. Help me lift my eyes to see you, open my ears to hear you. Give me chances, great and small, to become your poetry. I pray for divine wisdom and a deep understanding of how you genuinely hold onto me. Your word tells me that if I believe and do not doubt my heart, I can ask for anything and do not doubt, it will be done for me—words straight from Jesus' lips. Increase my faith to believe. I give you permission to, at any time, change my plans. Interrupt the direction of my life for your most excellent plans. My heart desires your will alone in my life. In Jesus' name, I pray. Amen.

You cannot go with Him and stay the same. Selah

What comes next?

If this book made an impact on you, please share by gifting another person with a copy, or by leaving a review at www.tonyaraines.com.

When you are ready to take the next step in your faith journey consider one of these online courses:

REVIVALIST BOOT CAMP

God wants to set you up to discover how you can impact and influence your community. Join me online—or in a city near you—to learn how to disrupt your city with the Love of God. You will master how to fully embrace a kingdom mindset, dream again, and discover your divine purpose.

DOMESTIC MISSIONARY TRAINING

Your calling needs to be activated because your city needs what you carry. If you feel called to a city and want to learn how to live out your calling, our activation-based training and coaching will equip you for success. Take the deep dive into your calling, learn more about hearing God's voice for yourself, and discover innovative ways to serve your city.

Visit www.tonyaraines.com for more details.